No. 2072
$11.95

HOW TO COLLECT AND RESTORE
PRE-WWII CARS

BY OREST LAZAROWICH

MODERN AUTOMOTIVE SERIES

TAB BOOKS Inc.

BLUE RIDGE SUMMIT, PA. 17214

FIRST EDITION

FIRST PRINTING

Copyright © 1981 by TAB BOOKS Inc.

Printed in the United States of America

Library of Congress Cataloging in Publication Data

Lazarowich, Orest.
    How to collect and restore pre-WW II cars.

    Includes index.
    1. Automobiles—Restoration. 2. Automobiles—Collectors and collecting. I. Title.
TL152.2.L39   629.28'722   80-28673
ISBN 0-8306-9622-9
ISBN 0-8306-2072-9 (pbk.)

Cover photo of a 1905 Peerless Model 9 courtesy of Richard A. Teague.

Contents

Introduction

The secret dream of every vintage car addict is to find a barn full of automobile treasures owned by a little old lady who is willing to sell them to someone who will care for them. Such things can happen, but most of us will have to be content with picking up the pieces where we can find them and slowly putting a car together.

The main purpose of this book is to help you put a car together. Whether you do it to save money, to relax or for the challenge of it, this book will help you do a better job. In the early days, it was the bicycle repairman or blacksmith who helped the motorist. The mechanics of the early days were mostly self-trained and gained their knowledge from books and trial and error experiences while on the job. The tools and equipment were, in many cases, made by the mechanic. These tradesmen now are hard to find so it's back to the days of the weekend tinkerers.

The application of the internal combustion engine to the propulsion of a motor vehicle has been one of the most important applications of our time. At one time, the automotive field was so new that all repair processess were in the formative period. That is no longer true. There are hundreds of repair operations which are standardized. It is these operations that I will be describing.

The automobile can be divided into the body and the chassis. The body gives the car its finished appearance and provides protection for the occupants. The chassis is a complete operating unit which can be driven under its own power. It does not include the body parts.

5

This book describes how to rebuild a chassis, but generally it is a book on the appreciation of an old automobile. Whether you do it yourself will depend not only on the amount of money you have for restoration, but whether you have the time and ability to do it. There is no way that you can do it all yourself because of the specialized techniques that are involved. You would have to be everything from a foundryman to a wheelwright and the time involved would prevent you from doing anything else.

However, there are many things that you can do that will go a long way toward the restoration of the car. Labor is the one thing that you must have plenty of because with it you will be able to do many of the services I will describe. You must also be able to recognize when to leave certain tasks for the tradesmen.

Good rebuildable cars are getting harder to find. It's not just a case of replacing the tires and the coolant. The "basket case" is becoming more common and the standards for restoration are getting higher. If you decide to restore an uncommon make, you will have to hunt in junkyards, farmyards and old garages to complete your project. For the more common makes, a whole industry has grown up around us and almost everything is available to completely rebuild a car.

As the years go by, it will become harder to restore a pre-WWII car to 100 percent authenticity. If we don't continue to do something now, there won't be very much left for the future. Perhaps in years to come, the only place where we will see a pre-WWII will be in the hands of the rebuilders. The cars we rebuild now will stand on their own merits for all to enjoy.

Orest Lazarowich

Chapter 1

Acquisition and Ownership

Car collecting has come of age. It is now as ordinary as collecting art, coins, stamps or antique glass. Depending on your interest, you might collect for pleasure, for profit, for the challenge of early motoring, for your own personal enjoyment or for a look back in history. If you don't have room for the actual cars, then maybe you are interested in sales catalogs, hubcaps, hood emblems, license plates or scale models finished to a "T."

Seeking Out

Unless you have a secret love affair with a certain type of car, the hardest and toughest decision you will have to make is deciding on the year, body style and make of car that you want to own or restore. Although classifications vary, most cars fall into the following categories: antiques, classics, general interest and postwar. The range is very wide. With the exception of the classics, there are many cars around at a fair purchase price.

Go to museums and car shows where you will see the display of many fine cars and note what interests you. Visit the various car clubs in your area and get to know the owners of cars that interest you. Write to the major clubs. If one particular marque fascinates you, find out something about its history and the possibility of restoring or finding one.

What you will have to spend depends on the make, age, rarity and condition of the car. As a first car, one of the early Fords (T or A) is the easiest to find and restore because there were so many built and parts are readily available for them. This make also has much written material in the way of reprints and major club articles. Even with a basket case, you will come out with a pretty good car (Fig. 1-1).

You will also have to decide on the purpose of your purchase. If you are buying for transportation, rather than for touring and club activities you are looking for a completely different car. If you want concourse competition, you must be prepared to bring your car back to a state of perfection. It is possible to own one car that will fulfill all of the above needs, but you will have to pay the top price. In addition, you will miss out on the pleasures of restoring your own car. When you make your choice stick to it. You will find that it is better to own a car that you like rather than one you bought because of its price or convenience.

Start by advertising in the local newspapers and the club newsletters. This method will save you a lot of time and money. Let the sellers come to you. Check with dealers and other collectors to see if they have what you want or know someone who has. If you are shopping from photographs, remember that photos are somewhat like lipstick and paint; they may make a girl what she ain't. See the car *before* you buy it.

Check estate sales and ask members of your family if they can remember anyone with old cars. Stop at the older garages and ask around and then track down the leads. There are still many old cars around, but people sometimes forget about them.

It seems unlikely that you will come across a mint car in an old barn or garage and be asked to take it away for $5. Most people have a fair idea of the value of what they are selling. If you have inspected enough cars, you will know the price range of what you are buying. The final price will be what you are prepared to pay and what the seller is willing to accept. Be fair. Don't take advantage of someone because you might find yourself in court paying a lot more than you ever expected. On the other hand, if someone is trying to rip you off just tip your hat and slowly drive away. There are many more cars out there and another will come along.

Checking Out

All cars are restorable. Some require a minium of expense and others take a long time and a considerable amount of money. This book will help you cut the cost of labor and show you how to do various operations with a minimum amount of skill. If the car you want is what is called a "basket case," meaning that it has not run for many years, the body is rotted away and most of the parts are missing, you should probably stay away from it until you gain some experience in restoring a car that is not in such bad condition (Fig. 1-2). But if you want to restore this car fine.

Find someone in the car clubs who has restored a similar car and respect his time and opinions. His help will be invaluable to you especially if you can get him to look at the car. If an inspection by another person is not possible, good written information will be important for you later on in your restoration.

Be careful if you purchase a car called a *parts car*. It not only causes a storage problem, but it probably will have the same parts missing and it might be in no better shape than the car you have. You will be better off by advertising for the parts you need or rebuilding what you have rather than driving all over picking up someone else's junk. Your time and money is better spent restoring. Work slowly and carefully and you will restore a car that you will be proud of.

I will discuss cars that are complete or with a minimum of missing parts. If you can drive the car, then the following chapters on troubleshooting will be of importance to you. If the car cannot be driven, for one reason or another, try to keep the following in mind. It is possible that a non-running car might be less expensive to restore than one that is running. Examine the car very carefully and see that it hasn't been pieced together from many similar cars.

Here is where someone who has gone the restoration route can be a great help. Look at the fit of fenders and doors. Open the trunk or check by the rear wheels to see if the quarter panels have been repaired and how. The only cure for rust is new metal and not fiberglass and screen. Remove the upholstery panel ahead of the front door and see if the front cowl has been repaired. Use a flashlight and get under the car to see if the splash aprons have new

Fig. 1-1. The Ford "Vicky." This is an easy make to start with because parts and information are readily available.

Fig. 1-2. A 1928 Plymouth 4-cylinder that is complete and not a basket case.

material or have been sprayed over with undercoater. At the same time, check the floor pans for rust-out. Check the outer bead on all the fenders and see if repairs have been done. Check where the fenders bolt to the body for signs of rust. Check the hood and firewall for fit and ease of movement.

If the car has been painted very recently, run your hands over the entire body and check for ripples, warpage and welds. Remember the saying about lipstick and paint. Your concern is to find a basic body that can be restored to good condition and appearance with a minimum of expense.

If the car has a lot of wood in its construction, you will have to get under the upholstery. For that you had better get the permission c⁴ the owner to do further examination. Shut the doors a few times and see what happens. Wood rot is similar to rust in that the only repair is replacement. Stand back and look at the body to see how sits on the frame. See a professional bodyman and get an estimate on how much it will cost to repair the sheetmetal and put it into good condition. This is very important because a chassis rebuilt to the best of specifications is no good without a place for you and your passengers to sit. Don't get in over your head; a bargain is no bargain if you can't afford it.

Further Inspection

Now let's get back to a non-running car and see whether it is a good purchase. Gauges missing from the dash are not too difficult to replace or substitute. If the block assembly is missing and with it the starter, generator and ignition system, these can be found. Radiators can be located or made up. Transmissions are not difficult to find and neither are rear axle assemblies. Front axles seem to have a habit of being made into trailers.

The next step is to locate the serial numbers or body numbers. Sometimes that can be a problem and especially if the serial number was on the engine block and the block is gone. Look on the frame near the steering box for any numbers that are stamped into the frame. Check on the door pillar and the door sill or on the firewall for any identifying numbers. Ask the owner on information regarding the model year.

With the information you have found and the support you have from similar car owners, start looking for the various assemblies you will need. Don't buy junk; it is only worth scrap metal value. Try and get good rebuildable units and not ones that are rusted beyond recognition. A quick test is to see if the assembly will turn over. In other words, when you buy a motor see if the crankshaft pulley will move. Check for external cracks on housings and blocks and check whether you could return the unit if internal cracks, etc. are found.

If you have to advertise for certain parts, remember to add in the cost of transportation. If you are buying from owners who have spares, see if you can work up some sort of a trade deal with them. Keep in mind that you will need the necessary nuts, bolts capscrews and washers to bolt all these assemblies together and onto the frame. Find out what you need and buy well ahead of time.

Make sure the parts you buy fit together in the model year. If you piece a car together, that is all right too because the experience you gain will help you in making a better car of the one you have. However, experience costs money. Sometimes it is better to spend a little more time looking than buying at the first similar part you see.

As your car is slowly being restored, the hardest thing that you will find to do is to keep your enthusiasm high. Try and keep a couple of areas going so that as you need parts for one you can work on the other. The weeks drift into months and the months into years and if all you have is a pile of parts its hard to get excited over that. Join a club if you haven't already done so. This is an excellant way to meet people who have similar interests and they will help push you through those slow periods. Do some reading and research about your car and keep checking the parts catalogs to make sure that the model year is right (Fig. 1-3).

When you need electrical parts such as a distributor, try to find the original equipment make to keep your restoration as authentic as possible. The same goes for the generator, voltage regulator or cutout and starter. It is these little things that put the shine on your car and a smile on your face.

The carburetor and the fuel pump are items where you should try for original-make parts. The many modifications made on these items alone should caution you to not just bolt on anything that fits.

Good wheels are hard to find. If you need them, start looking way in advance of when you want to drive. Wire wheels are easily restored if the wheel is not bent or the mounting holes are not worn through or out of round. Wooden wheels are much more difficult and you should seek out a wheel rebuilder to help you with part of the restoration.

Tires and tubes are readily available and the sooner you put new ones on all around the more pleasure you will get out of driving. Don't try to get by with an old tire that has been out in the weather; it just won't do. And don't put old tubes in new tires. We are driving on better road surfaces than before, so put something good down on this surface.

As you look for parts, you will find many accessory items that were built so that the owner could improve the car either mechanically or cosmetically. Everything from tire locks to luggage racks were on the market. If you are able to find something that interests you, by all means buy it. These items can even be collected by themselves. It is not necessary to mount everything that you find on your car.

So far I have discussed a non-running car with certain parts missing and how you should go about collecting the various

Fig. 1-3. A Chrysler coupe completely rebuilt and ready to go.

Fig. 1-4. It's easy once you get started.

assemblies so that you can begin restoration. If you have purchased a running car, you might not be stripping it down to the frame. There might be only certain assemblies that you will be restoring.

Each of us has certain limitations in mechanical equipment and knowledge, time and money. These factors will decide how much of the work you can do by yourself and how much you will have to get done by skilled tradesmen. In this respect, go down to the local garage or machine shop and make yourself and your restoration known. This self-introduction will help you many times over if you have to get any of the subassemblies rebuilt or even if you need some information on reassembly.

So go ahead and start and enjoy this hobby for the relaxation it can provide. If you can restore one more car so that other people can enjoy it, then you'll be more than satisfied (Fig. 1-4).

Chapter 2

Tools and Safety

Many types of tools are used in car restoration work. A good mechanic learns to use them properly. Using the proper tool in the correct way is the first and most important step toward doing successful work. Use each tool for the job for which it is intended. Select the right kind and size of tool for each operation. Do not abuse tools; they are but an extension of yourself.

Hand Tools

"Buy quality" and forget about buying the best you can afford unless it is the best. Starting with cheap tools will give you quantity, but as you keep replacing them you are going to spend a lot of money. Think about the damage that poor tools will do to your work and I think you will get the point.

Good tools are something you buy once and with care they will last the proverbial lifetime. In time, you will have the correct tool for every job and that in itself is beautiful. Remember, I'm not talking about the $5000 and more worth of tools that a professional mechanic accumulates. What I'm suggesting is enough tools to do tune-ups, minor repairs and maintenance of your personal cars. There is a big difference in the tools for a Model A and a Big Mack; truck not hamburger, buttonhead.

Get a service manual for your car and become familiar with it. Many of these are available in reprints. Get some grease on them and see what tools are necessary to do the various jobs. Learn that proper procedures prevent problems (PPPP). Top-line tools are expensive and they are rarely discounted to individuals. If you have some means of buying at a discount, do so and you will have extra money for some of the special items.

Pick up some catalogs from the main-line dealers so that you can see what is on the market and at what cost. Go directly to the retail outlets where you can see and handle the tools. Look for the stamp: "FORGED." This process produces a top-line product. The better tools are made of high-strength alloy steel and as such can be made thin without a lot of weight and bulk. This quality alloy gives greater tool strength and makes it possible for the manufacturer to offer a good guarantee on his product. Examine the tools for finish and bolt fit. The sharp edges should be removed and the tool polished so that it is easy to clean and comfortable to use. Heavy, bulky tools are useless on many jobs.

Ask about the guarantee and how it is handled. The better tool lines offer efficient repair service where you can get replacement parts so that the tool does not have to be discarded because of wear. Regarding tool breakage, check to see if they have to go back to the factory for examination before they are replaced. This could take some time. And what will you use in the meantime? Try and have the broken tool replaced where you purchased it and remember that most countermen know something about leverage and probably don't want to hear your story of it.

Try not to buy large sets of tools unless you are going to use every one of them. Check the price against individual tools and see which way is cheaper. You don't need a lot of carrying cases and that is about all you will get. Look around at what you already own and try to add to it. You might already have a hammer, pliers, a putty knife, screwdrivers and some small electric tools. You will probably never stop buying tools because as your car purchases change so will some of the tools which are necessary to do your own work.

The socket and handle wrench is the most common tool and it should be used wherever possible. The drive ends are available in four different sizes:

●The one-fourth inch wrench for small light work, machine screws and such.

●The three-eights inch wrench for nuts and bolts up to three-eights of an inch in diameter.

●The one-half inch wrench for nuts and bolts up to nine-sixteenths of an inch in diameter.

●The three-fourth inch wrench for bolt sizes larger than nine-sixteenths of an inch in diameter.

Sockets are made with either single or double hexagonal positions and are standard or deep lengths. The opening in the socket is made to fit over the hexagonal shape of a bolt head or nut. Sockets are provided with various types of handles and extensions to provide convenient working positions.

Some of the more common sockets are the ratchet handle, the flex handle and the speed handle. A swivel or universal joint is placed between the socket and handle when the handle must be used at an angle. Flex sockets, a combination of a socket and a swivel, are available for this purpose. Adapters are used when it is necessary to join a socket of one size drive with a handle of a different size drive.

Wrenches are used when a socket cannot be placed over the bolt or nut. Common styles are the box socket wrench, the open-end wrench or the combination wrench which has an open-end on one end and a box-end of the same size on the other.

Pliers are a gripping or cutting tool, but they should not be used to loosen or tighten nuts, bolts or capscrews. They are made in many styles including diagonals, combination, needle nose, slip joint and vise-grip which may be substituted for the other types.

Screwdrivers are designed only for installing or removing screws. The length of the screwdriver should be in proportion to the screw head. Standard screwdrivers have flat blades that fit into the slots in the screw head. Phillips screw heads have two slots that cross at the center to prevent the screwdriver from slipping out.

Hammers are striking tools. The ball peen type is used for general work and the plastic or lead types is used to strike soft metal parts or finished surfaces which would be damaged by a steel hammer.

Chisels are used for such jobs as cutting rivets or bolts and sheetmetal. They are available in various shapes and sizes to suit the job. Punches are used to drive out pins and shafts or to align parts. The starter punch, the pin punch and the aligning punch are the most common. The center punch is needed to mark the work before drilling and it can be used to mark parts so that they will be assembled correctly.

Files are used to remove metal and they are available in various types of cut, degree of coarseness, shapes and sizes. Your choice will depend upon the kind of metal and the finish desired. Rotary files run by an electric drill are handy where a regular file will not work. A hacksaw is used to cut tubing and bolts. The blade should be of high quality steel (because it cuts faster) and it should have 18 teeth per inch for general work. There are two common feeler gauges. These are the flat strip for checking clearances and the wire gauge.

Check the list of tools in Table 2-1 for a comparison of what you can start with, what you have, and what you can purchase.

Fasteners

There are many types of fastening devices that hold the parts together on a car. You should become familiar with them and the materials used in their construction and the proper installation. Most of the parts are threaded and the two series of threads in common use are the coarse and the fine. The coarse (UNC Unified National Coarse) can be interchanged with the National Coarse (NC) or the older United States Standard (USS). The fine (UNF, Unified National Fine) can be interchanged with the National Fine (NF) or the older Society of Automotive Engineers (SAE) thread.

If your car requires metric wrenches, the above is of no importance because your thread size will be in millimeters (mm). Don't try to replace a broken bolt with one from the Unified Series. It will not fit and your chances of damaging a casting, etc. are about 110%.

You will find one more thread size known as the National Pipe Thread Series (NPT). This is a tapered thread used on pipe fittings that produces a leakproof joint when fully tightened. It is not a fine thread and you will need the proper threading equipment to repair it. Check the plumbing shops for help.

The coarse thread is generally used when screws are threaded into cast iron or aluminum because a fine thread in these materials will strip more easily. Every bolt on the car has a specific degree of tightness (*torque*) to which it can be stressed so that the parts are held without distortion. To apply this amount of torque, you will need a measuring instrument known as a torque wrench. These are precision tools and they do not come cheap. You should consider one as an early purchase.

You will not be able to replace all the threaded fasteners on your car with original stock. When you are replacing them, check the markings on the bolt and screw heads to indicate the tensile strength of the fastener. Steel bolts and cap screws are not all made of the same quality material nor is the tempering the same. No markings on the head indicates a low-strength bolt. When in doubt, use a higher-grade bolt as a replacement.

Table 2-1. Tool List.

Hammers	Diagonal side cutters	Measuring tools
Ball peen 8oz and 16oz	Needle nose	Feeler gauge (flat)
Soft tip Brass Plastic Lead	**Screwdrivers**	Feeler gauge (round)
Punches	Standard blade set	Push pull tape
Starting	Philips blade set	Steel rule
Pin	**Wrenches**	Combination square
Aligning	Box end wrenches	**Nice to have**
Center	Open end wrenches	Universal gear puller
Files	Combination box and open end	Slide hammer puller
Flat mill	**Socket wrenches**	3/8 electric drill reversible & variable
Half round	6 and/or 12 point	H.S.S. drill bits
Round	1/4, 3/8, 1/2 inch drive	Brake tools
Square	Deep sockets especially spark plug	Piston and cylinder service tools
Triangular	Swivel	Soldering gun or iron
Hacksaw	**Socket Handles**	C-clamps
Blades 18TPI	Flex handle	Bench grinder - buffing wheel
Tinsnips	Extension bars of different lengths	4 or 6" vise
Aviation snips	Ratchet handle	Tire and wheel tools
Cleaning Tools	Speed handle	Body tools
Putty knife		Tubing tools
Stiff brush	**Chisels**	Tubing wrench(s)
Wire brush	Flat cold chisel	**Safety**
Pocket knife	Cape, half round	Fire extinguisher
Wire wheel for drill	**Other useful wrenches**	Safety glasses
Pliers	Pipe wrench	Metal container for oily rags if
Combination (regular)	Crescent or Adjustable wrench	your planning to rewash them, but
Channel lock	Allen wrenches	you're smarter to dispose of them.
Vise grip	Torque wrench	container for solvents

Remember that even though the bolt diameter is correct for the hole, the threads must match also. To check this, place the new and old bolt together and see if the threads will fit into one another. Then try the bolt by hand. If it doesn't go on for a few threads, take it out and check both the male and female thread condition. If you take a wrench to it, you will probably strip the threads or break the bolt. This condition can and does happen even when the thread is okay and the proper torque was applied. So don't break out in a sweat.

If it is a bolt and nut application, it is faster to make a replacement with a new bolt and nut of the proper size and strength. If it is a break internally or the threads have stripped out, that does not mean that the part will have to be replaced. To restore the hole to its original bolt and thread size, it must have a threaded insert installed. This can be done at a machine shop.

Spark plug holes in aluminum heads are a common repair item. If it is not especially necessary to return the hole to its original size, then it can be drilled out and an internal thread can be cut with a tap to the next largest size and a bolt of corresponding size can be installed. If the bolt goes through a non-threaded part, it might be necessary to enlarge the hole in this piece.

To remove a broken stud or bolt, several methods can be used. If a portion sticks out above the work, soak with penetrating oil and grip it with visegrips or a small pipe wrench and turn it out. Use heat if it is safe to do so and expand the part and then turn it out. Don't be in a hurry. Work slowly and methodically. If one method doesn't give the desired results, change methods.

If there is no protruding portion, then weld a nut to the part remaining and turn out with a wrench. Sometimes a sharp chisel or punch can be used to drive the piece back out. Screw extractors can be used. Follow instructions carefully and don't break a bolt off because they are very difficult to remove. If you have the right sized tap and the proper tap size drill, you might want to rethread the hole using this method first. Sometimes shortcuts become the long way about.

To clean up an external thread that has only slight damage, you can use a three-cornered file to "dress" the threads or you can take a good nut that fits the thread and cut three grooves inside and across the threads to make a thread chaser. Internal threads are best repaired by running a proper size tap into the hole.

Similar thread series apply to the nuts that are used with bolts and capscrews and the nuts should be of an identical grade to that of the capscrew. The majority are hexagonal in shape with some of the more common being plain, slotted and self-locking. Self-locking nuts are not reusable.

Various locking devices are used to prevent bolts and nuts from coming loose due to vibration. Cotter pins are split-metal pins that are placed through the slots in slotted nuts and through holes in bolts and then the pin is bent apart. Front wheel bearings are a common place where a split pin and a slotted nut is used on the spindle to secure the adjustment. Lockwashers made of spring steel and having offset ends are used to create a locking pressure under a bolt head or nut. Flat washers are used to protect the surface of parts being joined and also to distribute the pressure of the fastening over a larger area.

A regular nut tightened against one already in place will prevent loosening and this is known as locknutting. When a steel pressed nut is used instead, it is called a *palnut* and the same purpose is served except that palnuts should not be reused. Some connecting rod nuts are locked this way. Sometimes wire is placed through a hole in a bolt head and then bound to a similar bolt. Flywheel bolts can be held this way.

There are many new locking techniques on the market ranging

from chemical holding to plastic inserts. You want to rebuild your car as original, but how can you use a better grade of fastener and not change the external appearance that you want? Old, fatigued fasteners are of no use if you ever want to enjoy our modern roadways. Do you know of anybody that has 50-year old air in his tires?

Safety Guidelines

Safe work habits can be the difference between finishing a restoration or the restoration finishing you. You must keep a clean work area. You cannot expect to be successful if you work with grubby tools on a dirt floor. The slightest bit of dirt or abrasive that finds its way into moving parts will certainly cause a problem. You must have a place to work where you will have room to store the parts you get rebuilt until you are ready for assembly.

You will also have to provide some sort of storage for the tools you have or in time you won't have any tools left. Identify them with a dab of bright paint or ID engraving. Arrange them so that the ones you use most regularly are the handiest to get at. Some type of storage chest on a mobile platform is probably best. A wall cabinet is fine, but not if you have to keep going to it continually. Here you can use a small tray that can be carried to the job with selected tools. If you live in rental property, it might not be a good idea to start attaching cabinets to walls.

Choose a tool chest large enough to hold not only your present tools, but also to have room for some future purchases that you will make. Keep your tools orderly and clean. Wipe them before you put them away to prevent rust speckling. Cutting tools such as files and chisels should be separated to preserve the cutting edges. Delicate measuring instruments should be kept in their protective containers. A person's tools are a good indication of his work. When you find dirty, broken tools, workmanship is likely to be of the same order. Be careful when using your tools. Don't force them. Pull on wrenches. Don't push. If the wrench slips, you will "bark" your knuckles.

Fire is a possibility in any situation. Do not use gasoline as a cleaning fluid no matter what your uncle says. Oily rags are a fire hazard and they should be disposed of or at least kept in covered metal containers. The most common type of fire extinguisher for gasoline or oil fires is carbon dioxide CO_2. Have one in your shop area and know how to use it.

Be careful with open flames or sparks around batteries.

Fumes from batteries are explosive. Battery electrolyte is a strong acid and it can be highly injurious to the eyes, skin and clothing. If you are accidently splashed with acid, flush the affected area with large amounts of water and bathe with a mixture of baking soda and water. Soda, being an alkali, will neutralize the acid.

Do not run an engine in a closed shop unless the exhaust pipe is connected to the outdoors with a suitable pipe. Exhaust fumes are poisonous and they can cause death. Provide plenty of ventilation by opening doors and windows. If you start feeling dizzy, sleepy and tired, head for the outside and be quick about it.

When you must work under a car, use stands to support the car and don't try to get by with a jack. Your next of kin will be looking for a buyer of all those parts you worked so hard to restore. Steel milk cases can be used, open top down, but forget about bricks and boards.

Try to get comfortable safety glasses and then wear them if there is any chance of eye damage from grinders, buffers and drills. They still haven't made a glass eye that you can see through. Ground all power tools and don't be tempted to break off the third prong. Keep a first-aid kit handy and treat all minor injuries at once to prevent infection.

Chapter 3
Disassembly

This chapter should probably come at the end after you have had a chance to troubleshoot the components that make up the chassis. However, it's possible you have bought a non-running car or one that has parts missing. You would need to get into servicing a bit sooner. If you have a single garage or double garage that you are working in, it is a lot easier to remove the body from the frame and store it aside. If it needs some bodywork, you can get it done at this time. Check with the body shop and see if they will take the body on the frame. Then you can unbolt all the running gear, engine, etc.

If you find that the frame needs repair, then the best route is to remove the body. Remember that you are going to need room for the parts and a car disassembled takes up a lot more space than one that is assembled. You will need some shelving and some tin cans with good lids to put small parts into. Don't store parts in jars even though you can see what's inside. They don't stand much dropping.

Use your camera and take a complete set of pictures of closeups and subassemblies. Not only are they great for storytelling, but they will serve in reassembly. Make written notes and diagrams of things you are not familiar with. It might be months or sometimes years before you get everything back together. And you know what your memory is like, don't you?

If the car was driven or trailered home, try to get it steam-cleaned or high-pressure washed so that it is easier and cleaner to work on. Buy some grease remover, soak everything and then use the garden hose. Don't forget to hose the driveway down when you are finished or you'll have some permanent reminders.

Steam cleaning is probably the easiest and cheapest way of getting the chassis dirt and grease off but, you can do a satisfactory job in your garage or on the driveway if you don't mind cleaning up the mess afterward. Buy a gallon of degreaser at an auto parts store and coat all the necessary areas. Let soak as per instructions and then wash down with the garden hose. If you want to use some of the caustic solutions on the market *read* the labels on the containers and *observe* the safety instructions.

Good restorations begin with the frame. You must decide whether you are going to remove the body or not. The cars of the 1910-20 era are easier to work on in this respect. You should be able to remove the body without too much of a problem.

Make sketches and take pictures. It is going to be some time before you mount the body back on again. My first car, a 1928 Model A Special Coupe, took five years to finish properly. It was comparatively easy to get parts for, but if you are doing a rare type then be careful about setting any time lines. Don't rush through any part of the restoration; it's just not worth it.

On most of the early cars, you can unbolt the four fenders, pre-soak the bolts and you should be able to reuse them. Remove the running boards and splash aprons. The aprons will slide out after your main body hold-down bolts are taken out. The hood and radiator shell can be lifted off and the radiator supports can be removed. Loosen and take off any of the wiring that will go with the body shell and use masking tape to identify where it came from or where it goes.

You can make the body as light as you want by removing doors, glass windows, the seats and floorboards. Disconnect the gas line and any linkages that go to the carburetor. Loosen or remove the steering column so that you won't have to lift the body so high (Fig. 3-1). Take the gearshift stick out of the transmission and remove the emergency brake lever so that they don't become bent or broken. Place two 2 x 4s—one at the front and one at the back—under the body so that it can be lifted off.

If you are going to store the body outside, it should be covered to protect it from the elements and animals. Keep all of these body parts together. If some of them need repair, check with the bodyshop so that the bodywork can be done while you are doing the chassis. Get three other people to help you and the body should be quite easy to move. If it seems secure, check for any bolts you may have missed. Rust doesn't hold that tight.

The cars of the 1930s and '40s have similar body mountings and fender fastenings, but they are considerably heavier and you

Fig. 3-1. A 1923 Model T chassis minus the body. Steam or wash it down before you start disassembly.

will need mechanical lifting devices to part the body and the chassis.

The Chassis

Now you can see the efforts of your cleaning. If you find that you are going to get into dirt and grease up to your elbows, you will have to do some more cleaning. Do **not** use gasoline or any other flammable cleaner. Now is the time to strip the chassis of its component parts such as the front axle, the engine assembly, the transmission and the rear axle (with or without the driveshaft).

Make some sketches of the mounting places and take a picture or so of the complete chassis assembly. Use some plastic containers and drain the coolant from the radiator and the block. Continue along and drain the oil from the engine and the grease from the transmission and rear axle assembly. Let these areas drain thoroughly and then screw the plugs back in so they won't get lost. Remove the upper and lower radiator hoses and loosen the radiator mounting bolts. Gently remove the radiator and store it in a place where parts won't get piled on top of it. As a quick visual inspection, if you see holes in the radiator tanks or core it will need repair at a radiator shop.

The engine block assembly will be the heaviest of all the parts. The more you remove from it the lighter it will be. Remove the water pump. Remove the generator. Remove the starter. Remove the intake and exhaust manifold and with it the carburetor. Remove the fuel pump. Take the distributor out and with it the high-tension wiring. This should leave the block with the head and oil pan in place. Store these parts properly because you will need them later on for disassembly and repair.

Check to see if the driveshaft is open or closed by looking for the universal joint(s). If you don't see any, you have a closed driveshaft. If you have an open driveshaft, you can continue by removing it. Examine the transmission mounting and see if it supports the rear of the engine or if the engine has its own mounts. If the engine has its own rear supports, you can safely take the transmission out. Check for bolts, both top and bottom, and remove the clutch inspection pan if necessary.

Don't let the weight of the transmission sit on the clutch shaft. Remove it by pulling slowly out toward the rear. Start making some notes on the type of bolts used and where so that assembly will be easier come by. Loosen the rear engine mounting bolts and the front support bolts. Unless you have some very strong help around, don't try to get this block assembly out by yourself. Hire a tow truck with a boom and have him lift it out and place it for you on a strong bench of suitable working height.

If you find that your car has a closed drive shaft, remove the universal joint cap. Remove the rear engine mount bolts. If there are any shims there, make a note of them. Loosen the front mount bolt(s). Use a boom to lift the engine up and pull it forward so that the universal joint will slide away from the drive shaft. Place this unit so that you can remove the transmission assembly from the engine block. Some styles will have a radius rod attached to the bottom of the clutch housing. Disconnect this first before you lift the engine (Fig. 3-2).

You should now have a chassis with only the front axle assembly and the rear axle assembly bolted to it. These come off fairly easy. With the steering column already removed, loosen the front spring mounts either at the U bolts or on some at the shackle pins. Disconnect the necessary brake linkages or brake lines. Raise the frame enough to clear the spring mounts. If the wheels are still on, just roll away the axle. The front of the frame can be put on floor level or supported as you want while you undo the rear U bolts or shackle pins. Disconnect any brake linkages and lift the

Fig. 3-2. The Model T planetary transmission was the forerunner of the automatic. Note the enclosed driveshaft in the torque tube.

frame off the rear axle assembly. Now you have to find a suitable place to store all these parts. It is surprising how much room they need.

Heated storage is not so important for them, but your own work area should certainly have some heat in it. You can work on these assemblies in the basement and bolt them on in an unheated work area, but it sure takes the fun out of car restoring. Let's not try and duplicate everything out of the good old days.

Make sure these assemblies are fairly clean on the outside. If you want to make them lighter by removing the wheels, springs, etc., do so at this time but also make sketches and notes regarding disassembly.

Authenticity Counts

If your licensing bureau requires the engine number as the serial number so that your car can be registered, you can see the value of restoring to the correct model year. It does not seem possible that an unrestored car would not have some replacement parts from different model years. The owners then as now wanted to keep their cars running. There was also a fairly large jobber

26

parts business. It is possible that you have a car that has been "pieced" together. There is nothing wrong with that except that if you are going to restore a certain model year then you must obtain the proper parts (Fig. 3-3).

Before you take anything else apart, you should get all the information on the model year of the car you want to restore. Because one book will not give you all the information you need, you must do some research on your own.

The best place to start is your public library and the specific material they will have on your car. Use their duplicating services where you can so that you will have some back-up material. If you come across a parts catalog, this will give you a pretty good idea of what was available from the factory as genuine replacement parts. Some of the antique parts suppliers have catalogs that might help you with your current restoration.

A tremendous source of information is available from a club that is devoted to a certain make of automobile. Membership will give you access to information written by owners themselves. There are also many commercial car publications. Check the newstands.

Make up a clipboard or binder of information so that you can document before and during rebuilding. Make a lot of sketches and

Fig. 3-3. The dashboard gauges for a Brooks Steamer.

Fig. 3-4. Take pictures at various stages of disassembly and make notes. Your memory is shorter than you think.

notes. Your memory is a wonderful tool but is very short. There will be times when your work has stopped temporarily for want of some part or specialized service, but continue along with other work so that you will have several things going at the same time (Fig. 3-4).

Be systematic in your dismantling and keep related parts together. When you get to the repair section, you'll have lots of time for inspection and assembly. Remember the old adage "Haste makes Waste." If you break something, it will just take that much longer to get your car completed and on the road where you want to enjoy it.

Chapter 4
Troubleshooting the Running Gear

The running gear consists of the frame, suspension systems, steering gear and linkage, wheels, tires, and braking system.

Visual Tests

Walk around the car and see if it sits level. If not, check in the storage areas for an unbalanced load condition. Use a push-pull tape and measure the height at the same places on each side. Check the tires for the same size and see that the tire pressure is the same in each.

Slide under the car and check the spring clips for looseness. Look for bright metal spots that indicate metal rubbing against metal. See if the spring center bolt is in place. To determine this condition, measure the distance between a locating hole at the rear of the spring-mounting bracket common to both side rails and the forward edge of the axle or axle housing. This dimension must be the same on both sides of the car. See if the springs sag. Have they lost arch and will they need reworking?

Slide a bar between the shackle pins and the spring and check the shackles and bushings for wear. On some models, check the spring perch and front radius rod for looseness. On these cars, check the front and rear crossmembers for cracks and loose rivets. Also check the rear radius rods where they connect at the driveshaft housing and at the rear wheels. If the shock absorbers are on or connected, see that they are not binding. Bounce the front and rear end of the car to check for noisy, weak, loose or damage springs and shock absorbers. Although only one corner might sag, check all four shock absorbers and springs. One or more binding springs might hold other corners of the car high or low and cause uneven weight distribution with resulting abnormal tire wear.

Check the engine and transmission mounts for looseness or damage. Check the suspension parts for loose mountings, excessive wear, cracks or damage. Inspect the steering column, steering gear and linkage for loose mountings, wear or damaged parts.

Raise the front end of the car and place it on stands. Rotate the wheels to make sure that they turn freely without the brakes or bearings binding. Check the bearings for noise, looseness and improper adjustment. Grab the tire top and bottom and move it back and forth to check the kingpins for wear. Spin the tires and check for runout by holding a pencil or pen against the rim edge for marker. Check the tires for uneven wear pattern and ply separation. Raise the rear tires off the ground and place the car on stands. Do similar checks for the bearings and brake shoes. Let the car down (Fig. 4-1).

Sit in the drivers position and see how far you can turn the steering wheel before the front wheels move; up to 2 inches is normal. Pull back on the steering wheel and see what up and down movement you have. There should not be any (Fig. 4-2).

Driving Tests

When troubleshooting a running gear problem, it is important to follow a test pattern before and during a road test that will isolate the area or item that is causing the problem. The reason for this is that several of the problems attributable to front suspension components are also common to steering gear and linkage, rear suspension, and wheel or tire problems.

Let me give you an example. Wrong or uneven tire pressure can cause steering problems. However, a misaligned rear suspension, a binding steering linkage or improperly aligned front suspension components will have a similar effect on the steering capability of the car.

Take a short drive over a smooth and level surface, a rough surface and a roadway with a series of small dips. On the level road, check for steering bind, side to side wander, looseness in the steering gear, shimmy, pulling to one side, noise, excessive front-end vibration and steering wheel vibrations.

Drive the car over a surface that has roughness or dips and check for wander, rough ride, noisy conditions, excessive vibration at the steering wheel, weak or bottoming springs and defective shock absorbers.

Perform a series of quick stops in both forward and reverse gears and check for excessive dipping action, bounce or bottoming caused by weak or damaged springs or shock absorbers.

Perform a series of slow turns to the right and left and check the steering mechanism for excessive play, hard steering and poor steering recovery. Check for excessive body sway. This can be caused by weak springs and a weak shock absorber or a loose stabilizer.

If you can use a large parking lot area such as a shopping center or even a wide driveway, turn the steering wheel fully to the left and drive the car in a complete circle and observe the diameter of the turn. Perform a similar turn to the right. If the diameter is not

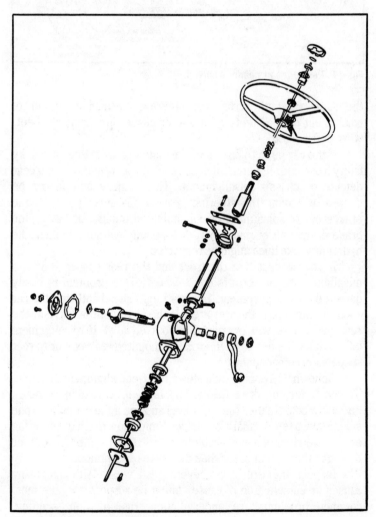

Fig. 4-1. Steering gear assembly.

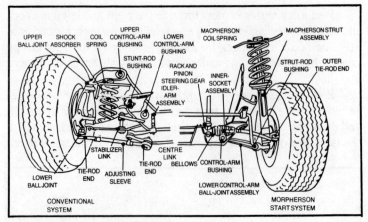

Fig. 4-2. Two common steering systems.

the same on both turns, the steering mechanism is out of adjustment or the steering linkage or suspension arms are bent, worn or damaged.

If the car pulls to one side, the condition might be caused by faulty front-end alignment, defective wheel bearings, steering gear defects or chassis misalignment. This same condition can be caused by having the steering gear in off-center position, the brakes out of adjustment or contaminated linings, or having the brake drums out of round. With cars using hydraulic brakes, the hydraulic brake lines might be restricted.

If you suspect that the front and the rear suspension is in misalignment, the term is *dog tracking*. This problem is easily detected on wet pavement. Drive straight ahead and stop the car about a length past the wet area. If the alignment is correct, the rear tire prints will overlap the front equally. If misalignment exists, it can be due to an improperly mounted rear axle or to rear suspension components.

Abnormal tire wear indicates a front-end alignment problem. To check this out, drive the car on a fairly level road in a straight line. Now release the steering wheel and see if the car pulls to one side. Make a few normal stops to determine how much the steering or front-end alignment problem is related to the amount or direction that the car pulls when the brakes are applied.

Inspect the tires for uneven tread wear. Although many causes or combination of causes might be responsible, the most common problems are underinflation, overinflation, scuffing, camber wear and cornering wear. When a tire is run underinflated, the side walls and the shoulders of the tread carry the load. Due to the low internal pressure, the center section folds in and rapid edge wear or shoulder wear occurs.

Overinflation causes the center section of the tread to receive most of the driving and braking loads. This causes it to wear much faster than the shoulder sections. Scuffing action produces a feather edge on the ribs of the tread which you can detect by rubbing the hand across the face of the tire. This is caused by excessive toe-in or toe-out and causes the tires to drag and rapidly wear away the tread. Check this problem immediately or you'll be buying new rubber very soon. Camber wear is evidenced by more wear on one side of the tread than the other. Rounding of the outside corner is caused by excessive speed around corners. One very common wear pattern is a series of cups and flat spots caused by wheel unbalance and wheel misalignment. This can only be corrected by complete front-end work, proper balancing of tires and most important, a new set of front tires.

Brake Systems

Cars use either a mechanical or a hydraulic brake system to slow them down or to stop them. Most cars are fitted with the service or foot brake and the emergency or parking brake. The foot brake is used for stopping the car and is applied by pressure from the driver's foot to the brake pedal. The parking brake is applied by a lever and it is used to keep the car from moving when parked.

When mechanical brakes, a system of levers transmit the foot pressure into an expanding action of the brake shoes against the turning brake drum to stop the car (Fig. 4-3). Each tire must be capable of creating equal friction at the road surface. Try to at least have your tire treads matched front and rear. Hydraulic brakes deliver equal pressure to each of the wheel cylinders and this pressure must cause each of the wheel cylinders pistons to move outward to apply the brake shoe linings against the braking surface of each drum with equal pressure (Fig. 4-4). Some typical problems associated with the service brakes of either system include the following: grabbing, dragging, fading and noise.

When one wheel grabs, the condition is caused by too much braking friction between the brake linings and brake drum of one wheel or unequal friction between the tread of one tire and the road surface. When all the brakes grab, the problem is with all the wheel brake assemblies.

Fig. 4-3. Mechanical brake system.

Remove the brake drums at the problem wheel(s) and check the brake linings for defects, contamination or the wrong type of material. You will find it easier to remove the wheels first and then the brake drums. Place the car on stands. Don't try to get by with a car jack. The front drums will come off by removing the outer wheel bearing and loosening of the brake shoe adjustment. Rear drums are a bit tougher. This is especially true for the style that fits on the tapered axle. With these, in absence of proper pulling equipment, you can loosen the outer axle nut a few turns and then drive the car through a number of right and left turns to help loosen the drum. Check all the internal brake parts for lubrication at the friction areas.

If you find that the brakes drag on all four wheels, the problem is one of adjustment on the mechanical system and a master cylinder on the hydraulic system. If the rear brakes are dragging, check the parking brake adjustment and the operating linkage. If the brakes drag at one wheel only, the problem might be adjustment, improper assembly of the brake shoes, a bad front wheel bearing or a restriction in the hydraulic line.

Brake fade is caused by an overheated drum expanding away from the brake linings after many hard stops. Any condition causing over-heating—such as riding the brake pedal, repeated panic stops, incorrect brake linings, glazed brake linings, thin brake drums and weak brake shoe return springs—will contribute to fading.

Noisy brakes or brake chatter (squeal) is caused by vibration due to loose parts or to misalignment of the brake shoes which prevents the proper shoe contact with the drum. When checking for noise, raise and rotate each wheel without the brakes applied first and then have someone lightly apply brake pedal pressure so that the linings will contact the drum. To check for chatter, drive the car and apply and release the brakes while listening for any unusual noises at the wheel. Brake chatter can be caused by loose backing plates, loose brake linings, oil or grease on the linings, bent or distorted brake shoes loose retaining springs or distorted or out-of-round brake drums.

Problems associated with brake pedal action are low pedal or hard pedal and a soft or spongy pedal. With a low pedal, the brakes might be capable of stopping the car under normal conditions, but there might not be enough reserve left in case of an emergency.

This condition is generally caused by excessive brake shoe travel in relation to the distance that the brake pedal has to be depressed. With mechanical brakes, check for the proper adjustment of the shoes to the drums. Hard pedal action with these same brakes is caused by friction at the levers or pivot points. Check for lubrication at all points. A soft pedal might be due to the springing of the brake rods. Check for the proper position of the brake rod retainer clips.

With hydraulic brakes, check the level of the brake fluid in the master cylinder first. To find the master cylinder, look either under the floorboards or under the hood on the driver's side for attachments to the brake pedal. If you don't find one at all, then you have mechanical brakes on your car.

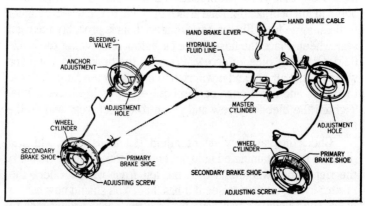

Fig. 4-4. Hydraulic brake system.

The master cylinder usually has an integral reservoir, but it can have a separate supply. Clean around the cap before you remove it. A piece of dirt inside can cause considerable problems. When you remove the cap, check to see that the vent is clear—don't enlarge it. This vent allows expansion and contraction of the fluid without forming pressure or a vacuum.

If the fluid level is low, it might indicate possible leakage of the fluid in the brake system. Top up the cylinder with only approved brake fluid. Do not use mineral oil because it will destroy the internal rubber parts. Replace the cap and check the pedal action.

If it remains soft and spongy, check for leaks by tracing the lines down to the wheels and examining the area in question. Check the rubber boot on the brake pedal side of the master cylinder. There should be no fluid under it. If you find fluid, the master cylinder is at fault and it will have to be removed and rebuilt or replaced.

If you find brake fluid leaking out at the bottom of the brake drums, this indicates that the wheel cylinders need repair or replacing. Any leakage along the frame or at the flex will have to be repaired by replacement with new lines.

Remove the master cylinder cap and recheck the fluid level. If it hasn't gone down and the pedal is still spongy, it is generally due to air in the hydraulic lines. This air must be let out through the bleeder screws in the wheel cylinders. The operation is known as *bleeding* the hydraulic brake system.

You will need an empty 8-ounce glass jar and a rubber hose 18 inches long that will fit the bleeder screws tightly. Fill the jar about one-half full of brake fluid and attach the hose to the wheel cylinder furthest away from the master cylinder. This is probably the right rear wheel. Place the hose in the jar below the level of the brake fluid. Open the bleeder screw. Press on the brake pedal and you will push the air out and it will rise to the top of the fluid. Release the pedal and try it once again because this is the longest line. Tighten the bleeder screw and go on to the left rear and do the same.

Check the master cylinder for fluid. If it needs some, add *new* fluid not the contaminated fluid out of the bleeder bottle. Go on to the right front wheel and then the left front wheel. Check the master cylinder again to see if it has fluid. You should now have a good, solid pedal. If you have to work the pedal a few times to obtain solid pedal, it might be necessary to adjust the shoes against the brake drums.

Two popular types of mechanism have been designed for adjusting brakes. These are the cam type and the expanding-bolt type. With either type, you will have to raise the wheels to get the proper adjustment. With mechanical brakes, undo the rods or the cables before adjusting the shoes and then readjust the turnbuckles for proper length.

Hard pedal action can be caused by any mechanical restriction in either the brake pedal linkage of the brake shoe assembly parts or it can be caused by a restriction in the hydraulic system. Remove the brake drums and examine the brake shoes for travel. Make sure that the return and hold-down springs are properly installed. Check the backing plate bolts. Brake linings that are glazed or have hard surfaces will also cause hard pedal action. Don't operate the brake pedal on hydraulic brakes with drums off because you will pop out the wheel cylinder cups.

Check the hydraulic system for bent or kinked lines that would cause difficulty in moving the fluid. Check the vent in the filler cap and the master cylinder itself for any restrictions.

Parking brakes that use one-piece cast iron shoes might be changed to a pressed steel shoe with riveted brake lining. External type parking brakes should be checked for proper adjustment of the band and that the operating linkage is not binding. On all these styles, check for dry friction points and brighten them before lubricating.

Chapter 5

Running Gear Service

The frame forms the foundation for the car and to it is attached the running gear. It must be light, yet strong enough to withstand the strain and shocks to which it is subjected. The length determines the wheel base and the riding qualities of the car. The frame projects a short distance beyond the front and rear axles depending upon the length and type of the springs.

The frame consists of two long pieces of channel section, called sidemembers, with connecting short pieces known as crossmembers. Small triangular plates are riveted at the points where crossmembers meet. These plates serve to keep the frame in correct alignment. Sometimes diagonal braces are used to provide extra strength and are located about midway along the frame and form an X or K pattern. With the body removed, you should be able to identify the type of frame construction you have.

Support the frame at a good working height and remove everything that is not riveted on. If your car has individual front end suspension, it might be easier to keep it together until you service the front end. The rust must all be cleaned off. Use any means at your disposal; a sandblaster is great.

The surface must be made ready for painting. Check all parts for breaks, cracks and loose rivets. You might be able to tighten the rivets, but if you can't they will have to come out and oversize ones put back in. On some models if the crossmembers are badly damaged, it is wiser to replace than to repair. Have the frame repaired by welding where necessary and fill any deep rust pits at the same time. Grind and finish smooth. If you want a first-class frame, you will have to do a lot of sanding, filing and priming to achieve that end.

Repair any of the bolt-on parts and if you reuse the bolts see that they aren't stretched. Measure the frame to see if it is bent or twisted and, if necessary, have it straightened. How well your restored car will look depends a lot on its foundation. Check the shackle bushings in the frame. If they need replacing do it now. If the frame has running board supports, make sure that they are tight on the frame. Build-up any elongated holes. Prime the frame and the bolt-on parts and then paint them with a good enamel. Bolt the necessary parts on. If you can get a spray bomb of similar color, spray any of the nuts and unpainted bolts. Set the frame aside so that you will have room to work on other parts of the running gear.

Suspension System

The wheels and axles are suspended by springs that support the weight of the car and cushion the road shocks. Springs must be able to carry the load without weakening and yet be flexible for easy riding. Parts supported by the springs are said to be *sprung weight* and the parts not supported by them are called *unsprung weight*. It is desirable to have a minimum of unsprung weight because the unsprung parts might be damaged by road shocks and their inertia interferes with spring action. Springs are made of special alloy steels. They contain chromium, manganese, silicon and vanadium to give them toughness and flexibility.

There are two main types of springs called the *leaf spring* and the *coil spring*. Leaf springs consist of a number of leaves of spring steel fastened together by means of a center bolt at the center and rebound clips that keep the leaves together when the weight is taken off the springs as the body and frame bounces. The main leaf has an eye at each end to fasten it to its support. The eye can be fitted with a steel backed bronze bushing or with a rubber bushing (Fig. 5-1).

When extra loads come down on the spring, such as when the car hits a bump, the spring tends to flatten out. This causes the distance between the spring eyes to increase. To allow for this spring action, one end of the spring is bolted to the frame and the other end is fastened by means of a swinging link called a *spring shackle*. Shackle bolts are made of special steel to give them strength. The shackle must be free to oscillate as the spring acts.

Leaf springs are fastened to the axle by means of "U" bolts. These "U" bolts must be pulled up tightly to prevent spring breakage at the center bolts. The most common leaf spring used is the semi-elliptical spring and it is usually mounted parallel to the

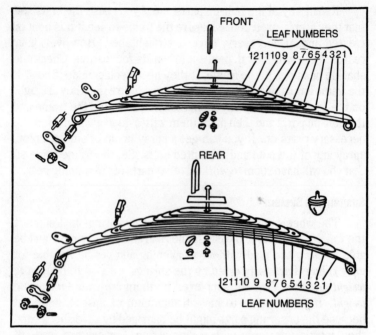

Fig. 5-1. Spring assembly.

side members of the frame. A few cars have a leaf spring mounted at right angles to the frame and are called transverse springs.

To service leaf springs, they must be completely taken apart because they affect not only the riding qualities but also the steering, braking and general appearance of your car. Remove the rebound clips and then carefully undo the center bolt. A vise is a safe way of holding the spring during disassembly. Broken springs or those that have little tension must be replaced or rearched. Check the cost here against new leaves. Remove the rust by sandblasting or with a rotary wire brush.

Replace the bushings in the eyes of the main leaves and if you want you can paint the leaves with rust retarding black enamel. Replace the center bolt with a new one and assemble the spring leaves as per model of the car. Use graphite grease to lubricate each of the spring surfaces. Coil springs consist of heavy spring wire wound in a spiral. The advantages over leaf springs are that they are active throughout their full length, there is no friction from coil contact, they need no lubrication and are quiet in operation.

However, they do require certain helper devices. Stabilizers or sway bars must be used to reduce body roll. Shock absorbers must be used with coil springs in order to give proper control to the more flexible nature of the coil spring. The lower end of the coil usually fits in a socket built in the front crossmember and the lower end is mounted on the lower part of the front suspension. Rubber bumpers are usually mounted on either inside of the coil or just outside to form a stopping device when a heavy road shock compresses the spring beyond its normal range.

Sometimes the shock absorber is located inside of the coil spring and sometimes it forms part of the upper control arm with the upper control arm working as the actuating lever. On coil spring suspended rear axles, special support arms, track bars and torque arms are required to absorb the forces applied to the rear axle.

When coil springs become weak, they will have to be replaced or retempered. Check the bottoms and tops of the coils. If they shine, indicating contact on compression, they will have to be replaced. To replace front coil springs follow this precedure. Lift the front end of the car about 8 inches off the floor. Place a stand under the inner side of the lower control arm spring pad from which the coil is to be removed and lower the car until it touches the top of the stand. Remove the lower pivot pin on the steering knuckle support. Disconnect the lower end of the stabilizer link at the lower control arm. Raise the car slowly with a floor jack and remove the coil spring. To reassemble, reverse the above procedure.

Shock absorbers are used to control the action of the springs in much the same way that a door checking device prevents a heavy door from slamming. They help to dampen the flexing action of the spring and give better riding qualities. Shocks can be of the single acting type where they control the upward movement of the wheel only or they might control the downward movement of the wheel only. When they control both movements, they are known as the double acting type.

Service on the hydraulic style of shock absorber is very limited unless you have the proper equipment. It is better to have them rebuilt or exchanged and then it is a simple matter of replacing them. Mechanical shock absorbers can be rebuilt at home somewhat easier, but it might be more economical to replace them with new stock.

If your car has a solid front axle, then both wheels are tied together by an I-beam. The steering knuckle is attached to the axle and pivoted by a king pin. A thrust bearing between the knuckle and the axle eye end permits easy pivoting while transferring the weight. Bushings between the kingpin and the steering knuckle reduce friction and wear. Rigid axle ends can be of the Elliott or Reverse Elliott type.

Other cars use the independent front-wheel construction. In this type, each front wheel is independently supported by coil or leaf springs or torsion bars. Because no solid connection links the two wheels together, either wheel can move up and down without disturbing the other wheel.

On all types, the front wheel hubs are assembled on ball or roller bearings. These in turn are supported on spindle shafts. The spindle shaft is integral with the steering knuckle which is supported by the kingpin or steering knuckle pin. On newer model cars, ball joints are used to attach the steering knuckles to the control arms.

To replace the kingpins on a solid type axle, you will find that it is easier to remove the axle from the spring assembly first if you have not previously done so. Take the wheels and hubs off and remove the brake backing plates. Undo the connecting tie rod ends and set these parts aside for further inspection and repair. If you find that the kingpin is seized in either the axle or the steering knuckle, have it pressed out.

Have the kingpin holes checked for alignment and straighten the axle if necessary (cold technique). Secure a complete kingpin and bushing kit and have the new bushings pressed into the front steering spindles. Ream the bushings so that the kingpins will fit properly. Install new spindle thrust bearings and shims and secure the kingpin to the axle.

Axles that have spring perches which are worn should have the perches replaced or repaired. The perch must be a tight fit in the axle. This style of axle also uses a front radius rod (wishbone). If the ball at the rear is worn oval, it must be built-up round. The radius rod must also fit tight into the front spring perches.

To remove the worn kingpins on independent front wheel suspension when the kingpin is tight in the steering knuckle support, you will have to remove the steering knuckle support from the upper and lower control arms. This will require the removal of the steering geometry adjustment bolts and that means the front-end will have to be realigned.

Remove the spring for safety. Replace the bushings and have them reamed for the new kingpin. Replace the steering knuckle supports in their respective sides and replace any other worn parts such as upper and lower pivot pins, inner pivot shafts and stabilizer linkage. There are a lot of parts with this type of suspension. Examine everything if you want good steering.

If your car uses ball joints, they first must be disconnected at the upper and lower locations and driven out. Again, it is a good idea to remove the coil spring. The ball joint itself is held either by rivets which must be drilled out or by bolts which can be removed so that the ball joint can be replaced.

Examine the upper and lower pivots and replace as necessary. Wash the front wheel hubs and the bearing assemblies and examine the bearings and the cups. The bearing cup is the part pressed into the hub and the cones slide over the spindle. A grease retainer or oil seal is pressed into the hub to prevent the lubricating grease from leaking out and soaking into the brake lining.

Oil the bearings lightly and inspect the cup and cone for cracks. Slowly rotate the cone and check for pits or chips. If dirt is still present, rewash the bearing. Do *not* spin a bearing with air pressure. Hold the cage to the center ring and let the air blow through.

Examine the wear pattern in the cup to see if the balls or rollers are centering. If any part cone or cup or rolling elements are damaged, the entire bearing must be replaced. Do *not* replace a part of a bearing. Use an approved grease and place a small amount on the palm of one hand. Scrape grease into the bearing until it comes out of the top. Make sure the bearing is completely packed with grease. Pack all four bearings. If you are not assembling at this point, wrap them in a cloth and set them aside. If the seals are damaged, order new ones so that they will be ready when you need them.

Steering Gear And Linkage

The steering system provides a means of guiding the car by turning the front wheels with respect to the rest of the car. At the bottom end of the shaft which holds the steering wheel, there is a worm gear. Meshed with the worm gear is a roller, sector or stud which is fastened to a shaft called the *pitman arm shaft*.

Fastened to the other end of this shaft is the pitman arm which in some cases moves back and forth or from side to side in relation to the frame of the car. When it moves forward and back, it is connected by means of a drag-link to the steering knuckle arm on one wheel and by means of a tie-rod to the other steering knuckle on the other wheel.

When the pitman arm moves sideways, it is connected directly to the tie-rods and thus to the steering knuckle arms. Almost all steering rods are attached to one another through ball joints. These permit movement in any direction. Some of these rods are adjustable to maintain proper wheel alignment. Check these points first before doing any steering gear adjustment or repair. If no adjustment is possible, the steering linkage ball joints will have to be replaced.

The steering gear consists of a reduction gear system situated in the linkage between the steering wheel and the front wheels. The purpose of the steering gear is to give the driver a mechanical advantage over the motion of the front wheels and also to provide non-reversal of steering when the front wheels hit any irregularities in the road surface. The four general types of steering gears are: the cam and lever, the worm and sector, the worm and roller, and the recirculating ball and nut.

There are two basic adjustments for most steering gears. These are the endplay of the steering shaft and the backlash between the worm and sector or roller or lever stud. Steering shaft endplay is noticed by excessive up and down movement of the steering wheel. Backlash is the movement of the steering wheel without any movement of the front wheels. Two inches is permissible.

To adjust for endplay of the steering shaft, remove the pitman arm from the cross-shaft and check the steering gear mounting bolts at the frame. Set the steering wheel in straight-ahead position by turning it all the way in one direction and then as far as it will go in the opposite direction—counting the turns. Then turn the wheel exactly half way back. Turn the wheel gently to avoid bumping at the end of the turn as the sector roller might be damaged by too sudden a stopping effect.

On some steering gears, endplay adjustment is made by removing shims—either above or below the worm gear bearings—and thus pushing the worm gear bearing cup closer to the cone on the worm gear and so removing play between the worm gear cone and the roller or ball bearings and the bearing cup.

On others, the cup is pushed closer to the cone by means of a set screw. Adjustment is made until it requires approximately a one-half pound pull on a spring scale hooked on one of the steering wheel spokes to pull the wheel through the straight ahead position (Fig. 5-2).

To adjust for backlash, locate the steering gear in the straight-ahead position and loosen the locknut on the sector shaft adjusting screw. Turn in to take all the lash and then retighten the locknut. It should take a pull of 1 to 2½ pounds to pull the steering wheel through the center position without it binding at any point.

If you find that you cannot adjust the steering gear, it will be necessary to replace the worn parts in it. Make sure that you can get the parts before you remove the steering gear from the frame. On some models, you will have to pull the steering wheel off the steering shaft and then pull the steering gear out the bottom. On others, you might be able to remove the floor boards and take it out through the top.

Use a steering wheel puller to remove the steering wheel from the steering shaft. It fits tight on splines or a taper with a keyway and key and the shaft damages easily. The steering column has a bushing at the top to support the steering shaft and it might need replacing. If the steering gear is already out of the car, it probably means that the steering wheel is missing.

Here you have a problem that has solved itself. Except that you will have to find a steering wheel if you expect to drive; vise-grips don't work too well. At least try to replace the bearings or bushings to tighten up the gears if you find that you can't locate a new worm or sector.

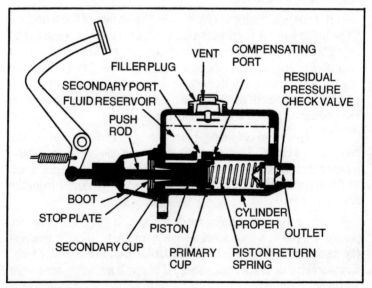

Fig. 5-2. Steering gear adjustments.

Brake Systems

Early cars had brakes only on the two rear wheels. Rods or flexible cables were used to operate an external brake band that served as a service brake. A hand brake lever engaged an internal brake using either an expanding brake shoe or band and became the emergency brake. The brake drums are usually mounted on the hubs of the rear wheels where an internal brake operates inside of the drum and the external brake on the outside.

To make the brake system more effective, four-wheel brakes were adapted. This type has the advantage of equalizing the braking strain on the four wheels, eliminating skidding, and making possible quick stops at high speeds with a very smooth action. The instructions that follow are for relining brake bands and can be modified for Ford Model Ts by using cotton belting and brass split rivets.

Raise the back of the car and place stands under the rear axle housings. Disconnect the levers from the brake bands and remove the wheels and bands. Wash all the parts to remove the grease and dirt. Examine the lining for evidence of wear and grease. If the lining is worn down so far that the band is making contact with the drum, a new brake lining must be applied. If the brake lining has worn down to the rivet heads, it should be renewed—unless the rivets can be sunk lower.

If there is a coating of grease over the surface of the lining and if the lining has not been worn out, you can draw the grease out by using heat. Direct a flame gently to the lining. Be careful not too char it. The grease will come to the surface of the lining in the form of a black carbon deposit that can be removed with a wire brush. To prevent grease from reaching the brake lining, replace the seal or felt washer in the wheel hub or housing.

To remove an old lining, place the band in a vise and cut the rivets with a chisel. Then open the vise about one-half inch. Set the band so that the old rivets come over the opening. Use a pin punch to drive them out. The old lining can then be removed from the band.

Secure the proper lining ready to apply. If this is not possible, purchase a roll of woven asbestos and wire lining. Get the rivets at the same time. They will be of the flat-head solid or tubular type. Try a tractor or truck repair shop. They will probably have what you need.

Measure the amount of lining that you will need by using the old one as a guide or lay the lining inside the band allowing one-half inch more at the band openings.

Rivet the two ends to the ends of the band with a buckle at the center of the lining. Force the buckle down with a hammer and a tight fit will occur between the lining and the brake band. In the case of molded linings, use small C clamps to hold the lining tight while riveting. Chamfer the lining at the ends to prevent it from digging into the drum. If it is necessary to counterbore any of the above linings, use the proper equipment and counterbore to one-half depth on soft linings and two-thirds depth on harder linings.

Linings for internal shoes are also available in flexible and rigid styles. See that the shoes are clean and not bent in any way. Remove any burrs around the rivet holes by filing. Make sure the lining fits tight. This will prevent groans, squeaks and chatters. Use semitubular rivets with heads large enough to fill the counterbores and with shanks of the proper diameter to fit the holes in the brake shoes and of sufficient length for setting. Chamfer back the linings on the ends to the center of the end row of rivets.

Examine the brake drums for scoring, wear and distortion. Replace them if they cannot be serviced by turning. Drums that are only slightly scored can be cleaned by polishing with sandpaper and oil. Wash the drum thoroughly after this operation. Drums that are turned will have to have the linings shimmed to assure full drum-to-lining contact.

Follow the manufacturer's instructions for setting the clearance between the brake shoe and the drum. This governs effective brake travel. Proper clearance assures greater lining life and efficient brake operation. Examine all rods and clevis pins for wear. Replace them as necessary because they cause lost motion. The greatest mechanical advantage is obtained when the rods are at right angles to the levers with the brakes applied. Check this out carefully.

All parts of the control system should be lubricated to insure free operation. The best relining job will not work if the operating mechanism is defective. Use a graphite type grease or make up a mix of heavy oil and powdered graphite. See that the shoes do not bind against the backing plates. Replace all brake shoe return springs that are weak or broken. A properly adjusted and lubricated brake system does not require additional return springs.

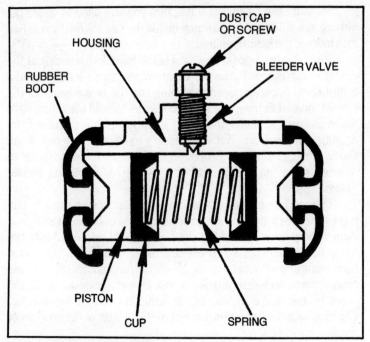

Fig. 5-3. Master cylinder identification.

In replacing brake rods or cables, be sure that the length is correct for proper operation. See that the cross shaft is not bent or twisted. This will result in hard pedal and uneven brakes.

Hydraulic brakes use a master cylinder to develop hydraulic pressure and can be vacuum assisted to reduce the amount of driver effort required to stop the vehicle (Fig. 5-3). The brake fluid is forced through steel tubing to the wheel cylinders in the wheel braking mechanism. The pressure of the brake fluid causes two small pistons in the wheel cylinder to be forced outward. This pushes the brake shoes against the brake drum and stops the wheel from rotating. When the brake pedal is released, the brake shoes are pulled back by retracting springs and force the wheel cylinder pistons inward. The brake shoes come away from the drums to allow the wheel to rotate.

Each time the brake is applied, a small amount of wear takes place on each brake lining. This wear increases the clearance between the brake lining and the brake drum. Therefore, the brake pedal must travel further to operate the brakes. When the clearance to the floorboards is under 2 inches, the brakes will have to be adjusted. When the linings have worn too much and adjustment is not possible, the brake shoes will have to be replaced.

Raise the car and remove the wheel and drum. Release the parking brake to remove rear drums. If the brake shoes are too tight to pull the drum, back off the adjustment. Some cars require the use of a puller to remove the rear brake drum. Before you remove the shoes, study the arrangement of the brake parts and make a diagram. If different colored springs are used note this.

Use brake spring pliers to remove the retracting springs and any brake shoe hold-downs. Do not pump the brake pedal while you have the shoes off. If the linings are held by rivets and if the shoes are in good condition, you might consider replacing the linings.

You can exchange the set of shoes for a set that has the linings bonded (high temperature gluing) and get away from the problem of riveting. Keep grease and oil away from the linings. Check the wheel cylinders by pulling the dust boot back. There should be no accumulation of brake fluid and the pistons should come out to the ends. To properly repair a leaking wheel cylinder, you should remove the wheel cylinder from the backing plate. Disconnect the flex line at the line connection and then unscrew the wheel cylinder. For the rear wheels, no flex line is used. Therefore, you must loosen the flare nut. Use a flare wrench for this and clean out any rust and dirt on the line that could cause the flare nut to bind on the line and twist the line off. Do not bend the line. Remove the wheel cylinders to backing plate bolts and remove the cylinder.

Keep all the rubber parts away from oil and grease. Wash all parts in alcohol. Cleanliness is essential. Examine the cylinder for scores and pits and use a fine grit wet and dry paper to lightly clean the cylinder. A slight pitting in the center is okay. The pistons must be free of corrosion, scoring and flat spots and can have a clearance in the cylinder of up to .005 of an inch. Use a flat feeler gauge to check. If the clearance is okay but the cylinder is still rough inside, you can use a fine hone to clean it up. The cost of sending this out might be equal to the cost of a new cylinder.

If you cannot get a new cylinder, you can have the old one sleeved. Use new cups and pistons if necessary and assemble in the cylinder. Use brake fluid for lubricant and make sure that the cups face inward on the open side. Snap the dust boots in place to hold the pistons. See that the bleeder screw is clean. Install the cylinder, connect the line and install the shoes. Replace any leaking grease seals and service the front wheel bearings if this is the end you are on.

Check the brake drums. If they are scored, you will have to get them reground if there is enough material on left on them. Do not weld or use any drum that is cracked. If the drum can be used without turning, polish out the glaze with fine emery cloth.

Drums that are turned will have to have thicker brake linings. See a brake shop about this one. Depending on make of shoes, some will need centering. Check your manual on this one. Self-centering shoes will not need this adjustment.

To adjust the shoes to the drum, have the wheel free of the ground. While turning the wheel, turn the adjuster in the direction that will expand the shoe. Continue until a firm drag is felt and then move back until the wheel spins freely. Do not adjust the brakes too close. They may drag, heat up and lock.

Since 1967, the dual or split braking system has been used. Before then, the single piston master cylinder was in use. Having only one operating piston, a failure of the unit resulted in total brake failure. With the dual system, one operates the front brakes the other the rear brakes. If one system does fail, the other will bring the car to a stop.

Not all dual system master cylinders are repairable. Depending on the cost, a new one should be obtained if honing is not possible. On single-systems, remove the master cylinder from the car according to the manufacturer's instructions. If it is very dirty, high-pressure wash or use clean solvent and then disassemble. Next, wash the parts in alcohol and see that your hands are clean. Blow the parts dry. Examine the cylinder for scoring, pitting and corrosion. Hone or clean up as required using brake fluid as a lubricant. Wash with alcohol and blow dry.

Check the piston-to-cylinder clearance. If it exceeds .005 of an inch, the master cylinder will have to be replaced. Check the ports; they must be clean and open. Coat the piston, cups and cylinder with brake fluid and assemble in reverse order of disassembly. Use a new repair kit. Do not reuse the old parts. Fill the reservoir with brake fluid and pump the piston a few times to remove some of the air. Install the cylinder and connect the lines.

Bleed the brakes as mentioned in the previous chapter. If you have someone helping you, the job will go a bit faster and easier. Remember to open the bleeder only when the pedal is built up. Let the pedal stay down until you tighten the bleeder again. Fill the master cylinder to the proper level. Before installing the cap, see that the breather hole is clear. Do not spill brake fluid on the paint. Wipe off and wash with mild soap and water.

Check the brake pedal for free travel. That is the distance the pedal moves before the push rod engages the cylinder piston. This distance is needed to insure that the piston will not be held in the forward position far enough to keep the compensating port closed. If this happens, there will be a pressure buildup in the lines that will keep the brakes on. Proper free travel for brakes without a vacuum assist is one-fourth to one-half inch.

Parking brake adjustment on cars using an external brake band can only be done when the lining is in good repair. If it needs replacing, proceed as with mechanical brake lining repair. To adjust, release hand brake all the way. Disconnect the brake cable. Adjust the cam arm so that the cam lies flat. Remove the anchor cap screw lock wire and adjust the cap screw until .025 of an inch clearance exists between the lining and drum at the lower half of the band by turning the lower adjusting nut. Recheck for proper clearance. Replace the anchor cap screw locking wire. Do not draw up tightly. Tighten the guide bolt locknut. Cable length should be adjusted to align holes in the cable yoke and cam arm. Install the

Fig. 5-4. Parking brake adjustment.

clevis pin. Use a new cotter pin. Replace the pull-back spring. This is for Chrysler products (Fig. 5-4).

To adjust the rear wheel type parking brake, first apply the brake about three notches. Adjust the equalizer nut until a slight drag is noticeable at the rear wheels. Release the brake. The wheels should turn freely. Lubricate the parking brake cables so that they operate freely. The service brakes must be adjusted properly before you adjust the parking brake. The parking brake must release fully or the brake linings will be ruined. Road test the car. It should stop quickly and smoothly without any pulling or diving.

If you do not want to do the *best* brake work possible, then do not do any service outlined in this section. Your life and the lives of others depend on a first-class job.

Chapter 6

Troubleshooting The Engine

The process of troubleshooting must be a well thought out procedure. It might mean the difference between a long expensive tow trip home or the pleasant time of a continuing journey. You must start by accurately determining the problem. Then you must use a logical approach (Fig. 6-1) to arrive at the proper solution. Don't be a buttonhead and replace the spark plugs when the gas tank is empty.

When an engine doesn't start, the problem might be in one of four general areas: cranking, ignition, fuel or compression. Each of these areas must be systematically inspected until the trouble is located in one of them and then detailed tests of that system must be made to isolate the part causing the starting trouble.

With electric start, the engine should crank at normal speed. If it doesn't, the problem is in this system and you should go on to Chapter 12. If the engine cranks, disconnect a spark plug wire or one of the connectors and turn the key on. Hold this lead about one-fourth of an inch away from the spark plug and crank the engine. A thick blue spark should jump from the lead to the spark plug or ground. If there is no spark or a very thin spark, the problem is in the ignition system; move along to Chapter 12.

The fuel system test determines whether there is gasoline in the carburetor. Remember to turn on the fuel shut-off handle and check that you have clean, fresh fuel in the gasoline tank or the vacuum tank if such is the case. On the gravity feed systems, remove the fuel bowl drain plug or open the drain valve. If you are greeted with water, change service stations. If dust comes out, remove the gasoline tank cap. If fuel comes out at this point, then the vent hole in the cap is plugged or you have the wrong cap. If the

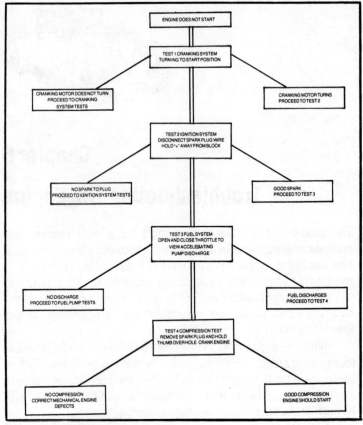

Fig. 6-1. Emergency troubleshooting.

fuel smells stale, keep draining it out. Don't smoke or try the ignition, you'll never make it to the fire extinguisher.

With the force-feed system, remove the aircleaner and open and close the throttle several times. Looking into the carburetor you should be able to see the fuel or smell it. On some carburetors, it will be necessary to remove the fuel line and see if fuel is getting this far. If you have no fuel at the carburetor, then the problem is in the fuel system. See Chapter 14.

If the engine will not turn over electrically or manually, the problem is internal and could be anything from a hydrostatic lock to internal breakage. Was there any unusual sound before the engine stopped? Did you notice any change in the readings of the oil pressure gauge or the temperature gauge? Did the indicator lights for these two go on and stay on? Was there any engine vibration before it stopped? Lift the hood and give the engine assembly a visual inspection. Look for oil leaks or coolant leaks. Check for a break in the engine block, or worse yet, a hole in the side.

Don't remove the radiator cap until you can comfortably put your hand on the top of the radiator tank and keep it there. When did you last check the coolant level? When did you check the level of the lubricating oil? If these levels are okay, but you can't crank the engine, you probably have internal breakage. There is nothing much you can do if you are on the road. Have the car towed home. Do not leave your car on the roadside.

It is unlikely that the engine came to a dead standstill without giving you some warning in the way of noise. These noises are generally referred to as knocks, slaps, clicks and squeaks. They are caused by loose bearings, pistons, gears and other moving parts. In other words, old age and thousands of miles have worn the engine out. Its tolerances have increased to the point where its appetite for oil is increasing and its vitality for get up and go has got up and gone (Fig. 6-9).

The engine is the most expensive part of the car to repair so pay attention to those noises. In general, most common types of noises are either at engine speed or at one-half engine speed. Those that are timed to engine speeds have to do with crankshaft, rods, pistons and pins. The sounds that occur at half engine speed are those related to valve train noises. Whether or not the sound occurs at engine speed or one-half engine speed can usually be determined by operating the engine at slow idle and noting whether the noise is synchronized with the flashes of a timing light.

A main bearing knock is usually a dull thud that is noticeable under load. Try to move the car under power with the brakes applied and see if this noise occurs. If it does, the clearance between the crankshaft and the main bearings is excessive and will have to be reduced either by the removal of shims or the replacement of bearings.

Connecting rod bearing noise will be the loudest on deceleration and should be the easiest to pick out. This is one noise you must tend to as soon as possible because it can lead to expensive repair such as a new block assembly. Connecting rod bearing "knock" can be cured by adjustment or bearing replacement if the crankshaft is not out of round or tapered.

Piston pin noise and piston slap are generally, the loudest when the engine is cold. This is caused by excessive clearance between the engine block and the piston or between the piston and

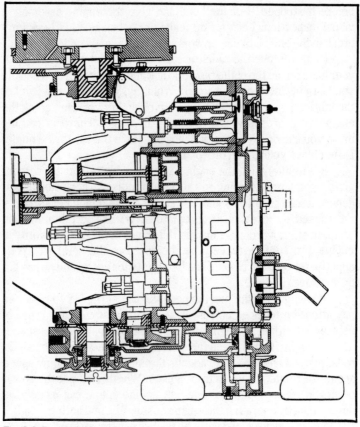

Fig. 6-2. Four-cylinder valve-in-block engine cross-section.

the pin. Pull the spark plug wire from the plugs one at a time. If the noise disappears, then it was probably coming from that cylinder.

The cure for this problem would be to replace the noisy piston. If all cylinders have this noise, then the engine block will have to be rebored and all new pistons will have to be installed. The rest of the engine is probably in similar condition. A complete overhaul would be the answer.

A loose flywheel will produce a dull click or thud. To test, idle the engine and then shut it off. If a thud is heard, the flywheel might be loose. Loose engine mountings might produce a similar sound, but it will be more noticeable when the throttle is opened or closed. Excessive crankshaft endplay will produce a sharp rap at idling speed and also at higher speeds. This should disappear when the clutch pedal is depressed.

The most common valve noise is excessive valve clearance between the valve stem and lifter or rocker arm. This is a clicking noise that increases in intensity as the engine speed increases. Adjust valve clearances to specifications. If the noise continues, it might be from other parts of the valve system or it might not be from the valves at all. Broken piston rings, worn rings or worn cylinder walls can produce similar noise. To test, remove the spark plugs and pour a tablespoon of heavy oil into each cylinder. Crank the engine several revolutions to distribute the oil around the rings. Replace the plugs and start the engine. If the noise is reduced, it might be the rings at fault.

You can use a long screwdriver or a piece of garden hose about 4 feet long to act as a listening device and help localize the noise. Hold one end to your ear and move the other end around until the noise is the loudest. However, a great deal of care and judgement should be used as well because noise travels through other metallic parts.

Oil and Coolant

If you find the oil level higher than it should be, it is possible that the coolant has leaked into the oil pan. If the coolant level is low, with no external leakage, then this is probably the case. It could be due to a bad head gasket, loose head bolts or internal breakage. Don't try to start the engine. Get the car home.

If you find that the oil level is nowhere on the dipstick, check for external leaks at the oil pan, oil pan seals, oil lines, etc. Have you been followed by a blue cloud without realizing that you were the cause of it? Your engine is trying to tell you something; it's burning oil. Oil is passing into the combustion chamber giving the exhaust gas a bluish tinge (Fig. 6-3). If most of your driving has been short stops and now you are on the highway at high speed and the engine is not in good shape, you are driving what is called an "oil pumper." The engine and the rings are worn and the oil is worked up into the combustion chamber (Fig. 6-4). Oil is also lost through the crankcase ventilating system.

The high speed means high temperatures and thinner oil. The oil pressure gauge is indicating all this with a low pressure reading. If you can turn the engine over manually, add oil to the crankcase and start the engine. If you hear any noises that indicate engine problems, shut the engine down. If not, you should be able to get to your destination with probably nothing more than a few extra quarts of oil. This type of engine will have to be overhauled before you can take it out again.

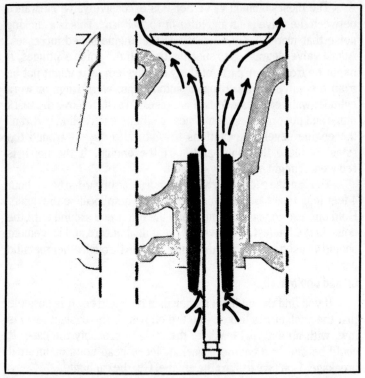

Fig. 6-3. Oil passing into the combustion chamber through worn valve guides.

If you have only a minor problem, it can be repaired en route and you are on your way. However, if there is major engine repair to be done it's better to get the car home. The cost of towing might be cheaper than hotels or you might consider a different car.

Compression

As I have mentioned, good compression is the key to engine performance. An engine with worn rings, burned valves or blown gaskets cannot be made to perform satisfactorily until the mechanical defects are repaired.

You will need a compression gauge for the test I am about to describe. You can rent a compression gauge for a short time. You might consider buying one. If you do, the one that screws into the spark plug hole is much easier to handle by yourself. If you have no gauge, you can use your thumb on the top of the spark plug hole. If the compression is so low that it won't blow your thumb off, then the engine is in bad shape.

You might also consider a remote control starter switch. This lets you operate the starter from under the hood better than using a pair of pliers or a screwdriver. Also, a vacuum gauge is a relatively inexpensive piece of equipment that can be very handy for isolating trouble in the engine. Learn to watch the needle action rather than the actual reading and you will soon be able to analyze engine problems. Full instructions are included with each gauge.

If the engine you have is seized, in other words it will not turn over, your next step would be disassembly and not troubleshooting.

Run the engine so that it will reach operating temperature and then turn off the ignition switch. Remove all the spark plugs from the engine and keep them in order so that you can analyze them later. Insert the compression gauge into the spark plug hole and crank the engine with the starter ignition off or grounded out. Have the throttle in the wide open position so that you will obtain maximum readings. Crank the engine through several revolutions to obtain the highest reading. Repeat this test on all cylinders and record these readings.

The significance in a compression test is the variation in the various readings between the cylinders. If this variation is within 10 to 20 pounds per square inch, the engine is normal. If a greater variation exists, then the engine might need rebuilding. Check the manufacturer's specifications to find out the proper engine cranking pressure. About 100 should be okay (Fig. 6-5). If low compression readings are obtained on two adjacent cylinders, it indicates the possibility of a leak from one cylinder to the other. This is usually caused by a leaking cylinder head gasket and this is a problem that you should be able to handle.

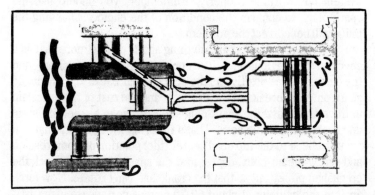

Fig. 6-4. Oil passing through rings into the combustion chamber.

If the compression readings are low or if they vary widely, pour a tablespoon of light oil into the cylinder(s) and take the readings again. Keep cranking until the gauge reads a steady position. If there is no difference, it indicates sticking or poorly seating valves. However, if the compression on the low cylinders is higher than before and about uniform with the other cylinders, it indicates compression loss past the pistons and rings.

By way of confirmation, carefully examine the spark plugs you removed from the engine. Check them to the cylinder you removed them from and you should be able to tell what has been going on in the cylinder.

A light grey color of the insulator indicates the spark plug has been running at the proper temperature. Any deposits should be dry and powdery. The hard deposits inside the shell indicate some oil is being used, but the condition is not serious.

A black sooty condition on both the shell and the insulator is caused by an excessively rich air-fuel mixture at both high and low speeds. If the deposit is only on the shell, then the low speed air-fuel mixture is too rich.

A very dark insulator with few deposits indicates the plug is running too cool. This condition can be caused by using spark plugs of an incorrect hear range or by low compression in the cylinder. Heavy deposits on the shell and insulator are an indication of excessive oil consumption. This can result from worn piston rings or valve guides. A wet and oil-fouled plug indicates a cylinder that has turned into a real oil pumper.

An insulator which is dead white or grey and blistered indicates an overheating or pre-ignition problem caused by over advanced ignition timing, a very lean air-fuel mixture or a cooling system not working properly. Remember, you should use the spark plugs to confirm the condition of the engine. Changing the plugs will not correct the problem.

Before you start taking anything apart, do one more test as a check on the previous ones. The equipment for it is very simple and the outcome is as positive as the post on your battery. Take an old spark plug and break out the insulator and the rest of the porcelain until you just have the spark plug shell. Braze in a steel tire stem and replace the valve core. That's it. Bring the cylinder that you want to check to the top dead center (tdc) position on compression and screw the air hold adapter into the spark plug hole. Block the crankshaft pulley nut so that the crankshaft can't rotate. Now force air into the cylinder at about 60-70 pounds per square inch (psi).

Fig. 6-5. Compression gauge used to measure compression pressure.

Listening at the point from which the compressed air is escaping indicates the nature of the problem.

Air hissing from the tail pipe would indicate a leaking exhaust valve. Air heard at the carburetor air horn indicates a leaking intake valve. If you hear air hissing at the oil filler pipe, the rings are worn. If bubbles appear in the radiator, the engine has a blown head gasket or a cracked block or head.

Now that your suspicions are confirmed, it is up to you to decide what you want to do. This will depend on your own experience and the tools and equipment you have access to. You will also have to look at your money supply and the cost of having the work done at a service center. If you have a mobile shop in your district, then you might be able to do some of the easier service and let the mobile do the rest. Some cars lend themselves to better break down of the component parts and you can take these in to a machine shop and have them serviced. In other cases, you might have to bring in the entire block assembly. Don't start any job if you don't have the necessary service manuals and the money to complete the operation.

Chapter 7

Engine Service

The major enemy of good service work is dirt. Even a trace of an abrasive on a bearing surface can lead to damage. Before you start any engine service, clean the exterior of the block. You will find it easier to see all the fasteners and on assembly the chances of getting dirt into the engine are reduced. You can use an engine pre-soak compound and the cold rinse or a high pressure washer such as a steam cleaner. Get the entire engine compartment clean. You will also stay cleaner. The day of the grease monkey is long gone.

Engine Removal

The majority of engines are pulled upward out of the engine compartment either with the transmission attached or separated from the engine. If the engine is to be pulled alone, the transmission must be properly supported to prevent damage.

With some models, you can remove the entire front fender assembly and radiator so that the engine block assembly is exposed. If you go this route, get some help because this is an awkward and heavy part to handle. Mark all the wiring for the headlamps.

If you leave the fenders on, use covers to protect them from scratches. Remove the hood and mark the hinge pattern if it is adjustable. Place the bolts back into the hood so that they will not be lost. These are a special bolt and might be hard to replace.

Drain the radiator and remove the hoses and the radiator core. Disconnect the battery or remove it if it is under the hood to prevent damage to it. Tape the transmission cooling lines. If you are pulling the transmission, start to drain it now.

Disconnect the coil primary lead, starter and generator/alternator wires, oil and temperature wires. If these are of the mechanical type, take care not to kink the tubing. Mark with masking tape for easy installation.

Disconnect the fuel flex line at the fuel pump and remove the air cleaner. To protect the carburetor, remove it and disconnect any of the linkages. Plug the hole in the manifold. Don't have a place for small parts to disappear into. Disconnect the exhaust pipe at the exhaust manifold. Clean the threads and soak them with penetrating fluid. Disconnect clutch and transmission control rods. Unbolt the front engine mounts. The rear ones will depend on location. If the transmission is coming along, leave the rear mount in place for now. Disconnect the speedometer cable at the transmission. Remove the transmission cooling lines and the container you were draining into before you knock it over. Remove the drive shaft and tape the rear universal joint together.

Drain the engine oil. Remove the generator and starter. Now, if you are going to work on the engine at home, build a suitable stand of convenient height that will support the weight. What I'm referring to here is a sturdy table. If you have an engine stand, so much for the better. Attach the lifting bracket and make sure the pull point cannot slip under the weight of the engine.

Check once more to see that all parts are disconnected. Remove the rear engine mounts on the block or transmission and support as necessary. Unless you have the proper lifting equipment, don't improvise. Not only can you damage the engine assembly, but the chances of hurting yourself are pretty good. Hire a tow truck that has a boom which will safely lift the engine out of the engine compartment.

Watch the lifting angle and change it if necessary. If you are removing the engine with the transmission, the lift angle is fairly steep. If you are pulling the engine, only let it come forward until the transmission is clear and then pull upward.

Raise it just high enough to clear the car and then lower it to a safe position. Remove the transmission and if you have made arrangements at a machine shop for rebuilding let the truck get it there now. If not, place the engine on a suitable repair stand.

Before you start disassembly examine your troubleshooting. If visual examination reveals a hole in the side of the block, you probably have a mess inside the block. If you have a cracked block external, it might be possible to repair it. If a rod is hanging outside the oil pan, be prepared to spend some money. In cases like this, try to find a similar block assembly or even a complete motor. If you can't, then you will have to make repairs if it is possible to do so.

If driving the car indicated that it is a real oil pumper, repair is possible if parts are available. Noise at the bottom end connecting rods, main bearings can be silenced with replacement parts.

Block and Bearings

Get some containers for parts and keep the related pieces together. It's a lot easier on reassembly. Remove the head. If the engine is of the style that has the valves in the head (I Head), set this part aside for now. With the block on its side, remove the oil pan. Check to see that you have all the bolts out before you start prying and distorting the oil pan. Turn the crankshaft so that any pair of pistons is at bottom dead center (BDC). You might find it convenient to remove the oil pump and oil lines to get at the connecting rod caps. Before you remove anything, see if the caps are marked to the rods either by numbers or markings. If not, mark with a prick punch on the side facing the camshaft. Use one mark for cylinder one and two marks for cylinder two, etc.

Engines that are seized are difficult to disassemble. If you can remove the crankshaft from the block, you might be able to drive the pistons out. Examine if it is possible to drive the piston down and out of the block. Spray oven cleaner on the exposed cylinder walls top and bottom of piston to help remove the rust. Use plenty of penetrating oil and let it soak into the ring area before you drive the piston. Sometimes it is a case of deciding which part is the cheapest to damage.

Back to an engine that turns. Purchase some Plastigage. Before you remove the piston and rod assemblies, check the bearing clearances. It is easier to do when you don't have the drag of new piston rings on the walls. Follow the manufacturer's instructions for this product and it will save you a lot of work. You can use it on semifitted bearings and the precision-insert bearings. See that you have the bearing clearances for both the connecting rod bearings and the main bearings and also the torque specifications. Use the torque wrench so that the Plastigage is properly flattened out (Fig. 7-1).

On most engines, the piston and rod assemblies are removed from the top of the engine. Examine the cylinder for wear by checking to see if there is a ridge at the top of the cylinder. This marks the upper limit of ring travel and must be removed before pushing the rod and piston assembly out of the block. If it is not removed, either the rings, piston ring groove lands or both can be damaged.

Use a ring ridge reamer and remove just enough metal to clean up the cylinder (Fig. 7-2). Work in pairs and remove the assemblies from the block. Replace the rod caps and if any shims are present keep them in order. Check the fit of the piston pin. If it is too loose, the bushing should be reamed or honed for an oversize pin or else replaced.

Check with a parts supplier to see what is available in oversize pins. The pin should not slide through when the piston is held vertical. Remember that you are taking the engine apart because it has a problem that you were able to troubleshoot. Look for this problem. The connecting rods must have the proper clearance or they will talk to one another. The main bearings are similar. The pistons must be free of cracks and the rings should not come apart in your hand. To make the engine block assembly lighter to handle, remove the crank shaft and the flywheel housing.

To remove the crankshaft pulley, you will need a puller. *Don't* attempt this job any other way or you will damage the pulley. Some models will have a two-piece timing gear cover. If yours has this, you can probably remove the crank shaft from the crankcase. This can be a heavy item so get help and lift straight up. You should now

Fig. 7-1. Using Plastigauge to measure bearing clearances.

Fig. 7-2. A ridge reamer is used to remove the ring ridge at the top of the cylinder prior to removing the piston.

have the block assembly either with or without the valves. Unless you have the proper equipment, leave the valves alone.

Visit a machine shop and talk to the shop foreman. Let him know what you have done and get some prices on the work that has to be done. This person's time and information is valuable so treat it as such. They will have to measure the block and related parts so get things in to them. Bring the head if it has the valves in it so that they can be serviced. Bring the head even if it hasn't any valves in it—meaning the valves are in the block—because it may have to be surfaced. Bring the oil pan along too because it is better if the machine shop bolts the entire block assembly together for you.

While you are waiting for all of this to get finished, you have lots of things to work on at home. Examples are the cooling system, the electrical system, the exhaust system and the fuel system.

If you decide that you want to do some of the work yourself, well that's alright, but the machine shop can still help you with the measuring and checking of parts. Don't get into debt by buying a lot of tools and equipment that you might use once. As your work progresses, you will soon know what things you need and know how to use. With the block out, you can get various machine shop service done to it and then finish it at home.

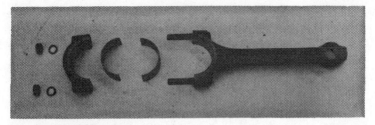

Fig. 7-3A. Connecting rod.

Other times, you might not want to take the block out of the chassis and you will do the various service operations right in the car. This is a case where a mobile machine shop service can help you.

One of the jobs that you can easily do at home is replacing rings and adjusting bearings (both connecting rod and main). If the block is out, it is a bit easier but it can also be done in the car. The two types of bearings are the direct bonded and precision-insert bearings used for the connecting rod big end and the crankshaft main bearings. Some adjustment is possible on the direct bonded bearings, but if it is worn the complete rod and bearing cap must be replaced if the crankshaft is still okay. The precision-insert type is not adjustable, but it can be replaced if the other parts are in good condition (Fig. 7-3).

This is where you go back to the Plastigage and the clearances it indicated. If you are only adjusting bearings and not replacing the rings, then the pistons will stay in the block and you probably could leave the head on. Do the main bearings first and check the crankshaft for any scoring, ridges or nicks. All journals must be smooth or the crankshaft will have to reground.

Fig. 7-3B. Integral rod.

Small scratches can be removed with crocus cloth. Use a "shoe shine" motion to prevent flat spots. Check the proper clearance with manufacturers' specifications but as a general rule an oil clearance of .001 of an inch for every inch of shaft diameter is satisfactory.

Direct-bonded Bearings

These bearings are adjusted by thin strips of brass (shims) placed between the block and the main bearings cap. Check the Plastigage reading and remove the proper number of shims to give the specified clearance. Remember that the bearing in the cap must be solid. If it is not, then the caps and block will have to be rebabbitted and the crankshaft probably reground. Also, if there aren't any shims under the cap then the engine is too far gone for adjustment. Do not file the cap. To try to get a clearance, you might end up with a far greater problem.

Start with the rear main bearing—that is the one nearest the fly wheel—and remove the necessary shims. Torque with new Plastigage in place, but don't rotate the crankshaft. Remove the cap and check the width of the flattened Plastigage with the scale on the package. You must have clearance. If you have had a problem with this bearing leaking oil into the clutch area, then you should replace the seal both top and bottom.

However, don't do it at this point, because it will cause unnecessary drag on the crankshaft. If the clearance is okay, loosen this bearing slightly and go on to the rest in a similar manner. When adjusting, try to have a similar number of shims on each side. If this is not possible, then have the greater number on the camshaft side. Use lots of oil and when all the bearings are adjusted torque them up and make sure you can turn the crankshaft completely around. Use either a socket on the crankshaft pulley or a flywheel turner, but make sure the crank shaft turns without excessive drag.

If not, go back to the bearing you last adjusted and loosen it off—then turn the crankshaft. If you find tight spots during turning, it probably means that the crankshaft is slightly out-of-round. This is not a good condition, but it can only be corrected by crankshaft grinding and main bearing rebuilding.

Before you go this route, consider how much you will use the car. You will have to do the entire crankshaft and the connecting rods also and this is a major expense. Leave the rear main bearing seal until you check the connecting rod big ends.

If you have noticed connecting rod noise and have been able to isolate the proper cylinder, you should be able to find the rod that is loose. Check this one first. If there is no bearing material left or the crankpin is damaged, then the repair is quite extensive.

Adjust connecting rods that have become loose due to normal wear and which have some shims left for adjustment. If you are doing this job with the engine in the car, have some means for turning the crankshaft. Turn the pistons down in pairs and see that the identifying marks are on the rod caps and the connecting rods. They should be on the side facing the camshaft.

A regular engine should have the numbers in order starting from the front: 1, 2, 3, 4, etc. But if rods from other blocks have been used, this might not be the case. This is no problem because you will be taking each cylinder separately. If there are no marks, use a punch or chisel to mark the connecting rod cap to the connecting rod. Do no mix the caps.

Start with the cylinder nearest the front and remove the bearing cap. Use Plastigage to check the clearance and then remove the shims as required. Remember to torque the cap each time. When the clearance is okay, see that you can rotate the crank shaft. To avoid extra drag, you can loosen off the connecting rods that you have adjusted while you are doing the rest.

If you don't have any Plastigage, just remove one shim from each side of the bearing and replace the cap. Torque and see if you can snap the cap forward and backward on the connecting rod journal by hand. If you can, take out another shim and keep testing until you cannot snap the cap by hand, but it can be moved by a light blow from an 8-ounce hammer.

Now replace one .002 of an inch shim to each side of the cap and retest. Adjustment should now be correct. If you find that with all the shims removed the cap is still loose, it means that the connecting rods will need rebuilding. Special equipment is needed, not only for rebabbitting, but also to check the crankshaft and regrind if necessary.

Check the torque on all the bearings. If locking devices are used see that they are in place. The crankshaft must turn. If you have made any adjustment too tight, you will probably burn out one of the bearings. Check to see which one is tight. Remove the oil pump and service it. New gears are available for some, but make sure that the pump body does not have excessive wear.

Check the inside cover for wear and use a file to remove any score marks that would allow oil to leak past the gears. Check the shaft for looseness in the housing. If any of these conditions exist, you should replace it with a rebuilt or exchange assembly. Make sure you get the pump back in properly. On some engines, it controls the operation of the distributor.

If you are going to replace the rear main bearing oil seal, make sure that you can get a new one first. If not, you might be able to shim up the old one. If it is necessary to replace the upper half of the seal, drop the crankshaft slightly by backing off the remaining main bearing bolts.

If the seal is of the wick type, use needle-noise pliers to help pull the seal out. Be careful not to mar the crankshaft seal surface. Synthetic rubber seals are a little easier to install, but take it easy. Work the seal around the crankshaft. Make sure that it doesn't bulge or hang up somewhere. Sometimes a wire attached to the end will make things easier. Pull around until an even amount extends from each side. Rotating the crankshaft might help. Now retorque the main bearing caps. Use a sharp knife to trim the seal flush with the block.

Install the new seal in the cap. If it is of the wick type, use a piece of round stock to roll the seal into the groove. Seat in the center and work the seal down and in toward the bottom. When fully seated, hold the bar against the seal opposite the parting edge and trim flush. Replace the cap with the necessary shims and torque.

Precision-insert Bearings

This type of bearing has a low-carbon steel back upon which a bearing material is bonded. New inserts can be replaced if the old ones are worn so much that the clearances are excessive. But if the crankshaft is worn out of round or tapered, it will have to be reground and undersize bearings supplied. However, if the wear is slight bearings can be fitted that will produce the proper oil clearance.

Understand what I mean here. The crankshaft has to be in good shape. If the bearings "go" on an engine, the rest of it might be damaged beyond repair. Understand the Plastigage readings that you get and if you have the use of a crankshaft micrometer then heed its readings. It is unlikely that you will find a high-mileage engine that has a crankshaft in it that does not require machine shop servicing. This servicing would include grinding, Magnafluxing and balancing.

Assuming you can get by with inserts only, do the main bearings first and then the connecting rod bearings. Cleanliness is the order of the day here.

Sometimes new inserts won't provide the proper bearing oil clearances and regrinding and the installation of undersize inserts is the only answer. There is a product that can be used to remedy this problem and that is the fitting of tapered shim stock under the bearing inserts. Consider this product if you want an inexpensive way of increasing the engine mileage.

When new bearings are installed, handle them carefully and keep your fingerprints away from the bearing surface. Use plenty of oil and if the inserts have locking tangs make sure they are in place. Do not file down the inserts and make sure the cap is clean before putting the bearing in. Torque according to manufacturer's specifications.

When replacing the oil pan, see that the gasket surface is straight and true. Use a hammer to repair the bolt holes if they are not flat. See that the gaskets and seals fit properly and use a light coating of grease or gasket goo to hold them in place and also prevent any future leaks. Don't replace the oil pan if you are going to do the rings at this time (Fig. 7-4).

I mentioned earlier the use of a ridge reamer to clean up the top of the cylinder so that you can remove the pistons without damage. The bottom end you are already familiar with. Remove the connecting rod caps, keep the shims and whatever in order and slowly push the piston up in the cylinder. A hammer handle does a good job.

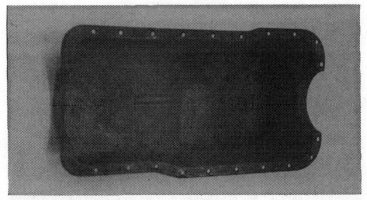

Fig. 7-4. The pan gasket.

If you have insert bearings, you might take them out of the rod and place them together with the connecting rod cap so that they don't get mixed up. In fact, you can take the bearings and tape them together to insure that they will stay together. Examine the rings even before you take them off the pistons. If they show irregular light and dark areas, they are probably warped. If the cylinder sides are scored or if they lack tension, they will need replacing. If they are stuck in the ring grooves or broken, replacement is necessary.

To remove the rings, hold the rod in the vise *not* the piston. Use a piston ring expander to prevent breaking the rings (Fig. 7-5). This might not be so important on the old ones, but the same tool is used for replacing new rings. If you break one of them, it is difficult to buy one ring or one ring set only. You can use your thumbs and forefingers to remove and replace rings, but be careful.

After the rings are removed, the pistons should be cleaned inside and out. Use a ring groove cleaner or an old ring sharpened to a chisel point to clean up the carbon in the ring grooves. This carbon gets very hard. If you have any presoaker use it. Don't take piston material out of the grooves—only the carbon. Buff the top of the piston only and not the skirt. Examine the piston for cracks around the bore and ring lands. Check the top of the piston for any sizing code, .010, .020, etc., which will help you when you are buying new rings. Clean the drain holes or slots in the ring grooves. If you experienced any piston pin noise, now is the time to check it.

Unless you have measuring equipment, take the piston and rod assemblies to a machine shop and have them checked or have a portable machine service come and make the measurements for you. At the same time have the cylinder blocked measured. I doubt that you will find a block that doesn't have some out of round, but the main measurement is taper.

This is the difference in the bore from top dead center to bottom dead center. The more taper the cylinder walls have, the more difficult it is for the rings to follow the changing contour and still provide proper sealing of compression and wiping action for oil control. Expanders under one or more of the compression rings and special lightweight and spring-loaded oil rings help provide satisfactory operation even with cylinder walls that have excessive taper.

However, when rings fail to control oil, and will not seal in compression, then the block must be rebored and oversize pistons must be installed. This is an expensive machine shop service, but if you are driving the car many thousands of miles each year then it is necessary that the engine be rebuilt. I think, as a general statement, that you could get by with an out of round condition of .003 to .004 of an inch and a taper of up to .008 of an inch. Check with the piston ring manufacturer as to what product he has that will help you.

For a proper ring installation job, the cylinder wall glaze should be scuffed by the use of a cylinder hone or glaze buster. The tiny scratches formed should make a cross hatch pattern on the cylinder walls to help trap oil and seat the rings. Cover the crankshaft to keep the grit off the bearing surface. If you are using a hone, force it down into the cylinder at a smooth pace and then pull it back so that the cross hatch lines intersect at an angle of 45 to 60 degrees. *Don't* pull the hone out of the cylinder when it is turning.

In absence of a hone, use an electric drill with emery cloth fitted to a shaft chucked in the drill. This will not true up a cylinder as the hone will, but it does scuff up the cylinder walls. Whatever you use, clean the cylinder walls of all abrasive by swabbing with light engine oil and wiping with clean rags. If you feel so inclined, you can use soap and water and then rub oil into the cylinder walls.

Fig. 7-5. To prevent ring breakage, use a piston ring expander to remove and replace rings.

Select piston rings comparable in size to the pistons being used. Piston rings must be fitted to the cylinder and to the ring groove in the piston. Slip the new compression ring into the cylinder bore. Using the head of the piston, push it down to the lower limit of ring travel. Measure the piston ring end gap with a flat feeler gauge and check with specifications. This should be the minimum measurement because it will increase as the ring moves up into the cylinder. To enlarge the gap, clamp a fine cut file in a vise and work the ring back and forth on the file with the ring ends on the two sides of the file. Fit each ring separately to the cylinder in which it is going to be used and keep these sets together.

Check the outside surface of the ring in the proper ring groove by rolling the ring around in the groove the entire circumference of the piston. The ring must have a free fit. If it is tight, check the groove for carbon or dirt. Now install the ring in the groove and test again for worn ring grooves. This is very important in maintaining engine performance and preventing excessive oil consumption. Use a flat feeler gauge. Service the piston pins as required either by using new oversize pins or by replacing the bushings and using standard pins.

To install the piston in the cylinder after the piston, rings, and rod are reassembled, it is necessary to compress the rings in their grooves so that they will enter the cylinder bore. A piston ring compressor is used. It clamps around the rings and compresses them into the grooves so that the assembly can be pushed into the cylinder without breaking a ring. This tool is really worth its money. If you've been lucky to date, don't push your luck any further (Fig. 7-6).

For protection of the crankshaft, slip small pieces of rubber tubing over the con rod bolts and carefully guide each rod onto the oiled crankshaft journal. Stagger the ring end gaps to prevent blow-by and flood the ring area with oil. Install the compressor around the rings. Make sure that it is tight. With the piston in the proper position and the rod number facing the camshaft side, hold the compressor tight against the block. Tap the piston lightly with a hammer handle to force the assembly into the block. If a ring pops out from under the compressor, *stop* and reposition the compressor. Failure to do this can result in breaking a ring. If you do break a ring, try one of the old ones and see if you can get a good fit.

Work the cylinders in pairs and install the inserts properly (if used) or the shims on direct-bonded bearing in place before torquing the connecting rod caps. Replace the locking devices. The crankshaft will turn although it has more drag on it now and will take more effort. Service the oil pump, screen and connecting pipes. Replace the oil pan.

Depending on the type of engine, the valves will be in the head or in the block. If they are in the head, send this entire assembly to the machine shop for service. If they are in the block, you will have to get mobile service for them or take the entire block assembly to a machine shop. If the engine is in the car, it is better to bring the service man in. Do not attempt this service if you are lacking in tools or experience. Grinding and seating the valves is a precise operation. Adjusting them is somewhat easier although some styles are adjusted by grinding the stem ends. Check what you *can* do over what you *think* you can do.

Fig. 7-6. Replacing pistons in the block by using a ring compressor to prevent breaking the rings. Use plenty of oil.

Valve lapping is a task which you might consider attempting. But unless the valves and seats are in good shape, you can't do much here either. Further service operations on the camshaft and its bearings are specialized areas. You might be able to service the camshaft gear or a timing chain replacement. If you do, make sure that the problem has been troubleshot properly.

If the car has hydraulic valve lifters and they are noisy, you might consider replacing them instead of servicing because of the labor cost. This is especially true for on a high-mileage engine. Study the shop manual before you attempt anything.

Now, let's complete the engine assembly. The head can be easily serviced. If the head gasket leaks, it is not difficult to replace. On the flat-head engines with cast iron heads, you can use a wire brush on a drill to get at the carbon. Check carefully for fine cracks on the outside surface. See that the holes in the block are clean and not stripped. You might countersink the threaded holes a bit to prevent metal from pulling up. Holes that are stripped will have to be repaired with a threaded insert (Heli-coil) or it might be possible to rethread to a larger bolt.

Check the head gasket for proper fit and make sure that it is facing the right side up and that all openings are clear and in alignment. If you are replacing a head gasket because of leakage, see that the head itself isn't warped and causing some of this problem. Sometimes guide pins can be used to hold the head in alignment while bolts are being replaced. The use of sealant is entirely up to you. There are many brands of sealant on the market, but excess sealer can plug small coolant passages—so take it easy.

You can soak the head gasket in water and then when you torque it down it will conform to any small imperfections on the block or head to form a tight seal. Run all the fasteners down snug in order as indicated on a torquing diagram. In absence of a diagram, work from the center out. First torque to one-third torque, then to two-thirds torque and finally to full torque. Improper sequence and torque will not only snap the fasteners and cause distortion, but it might cause the gasket to fail in service.

With over-head valve engines, you will have to bolt the valve operating mechanism in place and set the valves according to specifications. Remember to adjust the valves only when the particular cylinder is on compression stroke. Both valves are closed at this time. Some engines require that the valves are set at engine operating temperature. If you have problems setting the valves with the engine running, do them in two or three steps by bringing the engine up to operating temperature and shutting it down while you adjust the valves.

Surely you understand, buttonhead, that the engine cannot be run without coolant or lubricating oil while you are making the above adjustment.

If the engine went to the machine shop for rebuilding, you will have to place it back in the chassis before you can start it. Now is a good time to replace the clutch if that is necessary. If the transmission needed work, you should have done it before this time. Attach a suitable engine lifter and, using whatever means you have for lifting, place the assembly into the chassis. Replace the necessary mounting bolts and auxiliary systems and the engine should be ready for starting.

Starting The Engine

No matter how big a hurry you think you are in, work with care and caution. Do not use force. If problems are encountered, find out what is causing them and remedy them. I hope that in disassembly you marked some of the pieces, such as wires, lines and hoses, that you disconnected. Sure saves time now doesn't it.

I hope that you used plenty of oil on assembly because it takes times to get oil throughout the lubrication system and some of it will run dry for an instant. New rings can be damaged and so can the bearings. Pay attention to what you are doing and don't be fooled by a pressure reading on the oil pressure gauge.

Check the level of the oil and do not overfill. See that the cooling system is properly filled. Place fresh gasoline in the tank. The battery must be in good condition and if the engine cranks slowly use a booster battery in parallel.

Check the ignition point gap and try to set the timing as close as you can by the use of the timing marks. See that the spark plug wires are in the proper firing order and on their respective plugs. Check the valve clearance. Even the machine shop can make a mistake. Have a fire extinguisher handy and see that it works and that you know how to operate it.

You might have to prime the carburetor with an oil/gas mix while you wait for the fuel pump to bring fuel up. Don't prime with the engine being cranked. A backfire could cause a fire. The engine should start easily. If it doesn't, check some of the systems before you run the battery down.

Operate the engine at around 1000 rpm so that it will lubricate properly and reach operating temperature. Don't run the engine if the oil pressure gauge registers zero. Check this problem out. Inspect the system for any signs of gasoline, oil or coolant leakage.

Avoid exposure to exhaust fumes because carbon monoxide is a deadly poison. Do not run the engine in a closed area. Open the doors and windows and, if weather permits, run the engine outside. When operating temperature is reached, turn the engine off and retorque the head(s) and manifolds. Give the valves a final adjustment if needed. Start the engine and set the ignition timing and the carburetor settings. You can set the carburetor for a fast idle to get better cylinder lubrication during idle. Return the idle to normal after you have driven a few hundred miles.

Now take the car out for a road test and break-in run. Select a place where you can safely bring the car speed up to 50 miles per hour and then coast down to 30 miles per hour. Repeat this procedure for approximately 20 minutes. Bring the car back and check for any leakages.

Drive the car for about 500 miles and then have the oil and the filter changed. You might notice some oil consumption while the rings are seating, but this is normal and a normal amount of oil is used during engine operation. Don't believe that old story about "my engine doesn't use any oil."

Remember what I said about the other engine systems—such as fuel, ignition and cooling—being in good working order so that you will have top engine performance.

Chapter 8

Troubleshooting the Cooling System

Of all the problems you can encounter on a rally or during a parade, overheating is the one problem that makes you believe that if you can just drive a bit further everything will be okay. Don't you believe it. Pull over to the side and if your radiator isn't imitating Old Faithful don't make it do so. In other words, do *not* remove the radiator cap. Sit back on the side and watch the other cars go by smile and wave. I'm serious about this. Do not remove the radiator cap until you can keep your hand comfortably on the top of the radiator itself.

The engine's cooling system is designed to remove about one-third of the heat developed by combustion. If this heat is not removed, the metal parts will expand, the lubricating oil will burn off and the engine will seize. The cooling system must regulate the running temperature of the engine. Too hot an engine can cause preignition, detonation, knock, burned pistons and valves and lubrication failure. Too cold and engine can cause unnecessary wear, poor fuel economy and the accumulation of water and sludge in the crankcase. The cooling system must provide some means of heating the passenger compartment in cold weather.

The two types of cooling systems used are the liquid-cooling and the air-cooling systems. The liquid-cooling system is the most popular. With the liquid cooling system, water is used as a coolant and anti-freeze is added for cold-weather operation. With the air-cooling systems, air is ducted around cooling fins that are cast integral with the cylinders. Metal baffles are used to direct the air around the hot spots. A blower is used to aid in distributing the air.

Liquid Cooling

While you are waiting for the engine to cool off, raise the hood and do some visual checks. Check for leaks at the radiator and, depending on where they are, you might be able to plug the leaks and continue on your way. There are products on the market and they do a fairly good job on small leaks. A larger leak might be fixed by hammering a suitable wooden plug into it.

Examine the hoses and try to renew the leaking one if you can find a replacement. If not, use plastic tape out of your tool box to repair the hose. An external head gasket leak will be difficult to repair on the road, but if you can hammer in some solder wire where the material is missing you might get by. If your car has a water pump, check the packing nut for leaks and tighten as necessary. Pull the dip stick and check the oil level. If very little oil is indicated, you might already have an engine that is seized and your trip is over. Use the crank to turn the engine over. If you still can, then adding oil to the proper level might remedy the heating problem. If you find that the oil level is abnormally high and you haven't over filled, then it might be an internal water leak and the oil pan has water in it.

Remove the radiator cap and check the level of the coolant. If your car has a thermo-syphon system, meaning no water pump, the radiator must be well filled to keep circulation up. If the level is up and you found no water leaks, then you will have to do some more checking. If the level is low and the leak has been found, replace the coolant. Do not pour cold coolant into an engine that is empty and hot because you can and will damage the block or head(s).

Check the fan and see that the blades are all in place. If you have "thrown" a blade, you should have noticed it due to the vibration of the engine. A broken blade sometimes likes to go through the radiator. If this has happened to you, it is pretty self-evident.

You can drive a car with a fan disconnected, but you must keep the car speed up to drive the air through the radiator. Check the fan belt. It can get loose and the fan will start to slip, causing overheating. Depending on the type of water pump your engine uses and on its manner of drive, check to see if the pump is circulating water. Look in the radiator while the engine is running. If you cannot see any circulation, then check the pump drive. It is also possible that the inside of the pump is inoperative and would have to be taken apart and examined (Fig. 8-1).

Check the front of the radiator to see if it is plugged with dirt, tree fuzz, etc. See if the license plate or some other obstruction is preventing passage of air. If you painted the radiator fins with nice, thick, black enamel so that it would look good, you might have caused some of your overheating problems. The paint is not letting the heat radiate (Fig. 8-1).

If everything looks good under the hood and you have topped up the coolant, but it boils or overheats again in a short time, make some other checks. If the engine is new or recently overhauled, the bearings, etc. might be tight and have not yet loosened up.

Are the brakes properly adjusted? Did you raise the wheels off the floor when you made the necessary adjustments? If the car uses a thermostat, are you sure you replaced it with the bellows pointing down? Depending on the water supply in your area, does the inside of the block or radiator look like the inside of the kitchen kettle? This coating will prevent heat transfer from engine to coolant. What about the rust that forms on the metal parts inside the engine? This rust can settle inside the radiator and cut down the heat transfer.

If you are on a cross-country rally and didn't service the cooling system before this time, well shame on you. Without coolant in the system, do not drive the car. Have it moved to where there is a source of water. If there is a radiator shop nearby, then be smart and head for it. If not, you can try one of the cleaners for flushing the system without having to remove the radiator. Follow the manufacturer's instructions and take no short cuts. Remember

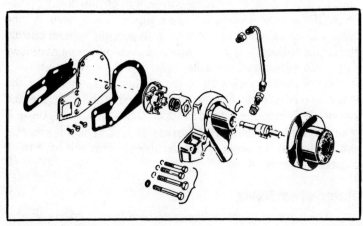

Fig. 8-1. A circulating water pump.

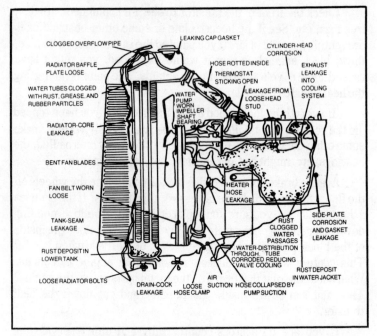

Fig. 8-2. Danger spots in the cooling system.

that you can only do this service when you have eliminated any of the previous possible problems (Figs. 8-2 and 8-3).

If the cooling system is clean and of the right size for your car and the other parts in good repair and adjustment, you will have to look at the areas of carburetion and ignition. Adjust the timing to specifications. Improper timing will lead to engine heating problems. If your car has manual spark timing, check your driving habits. Keep the spark advanced as far as possible without causing the engine to knock. As the throttle is opened and the engine slows down, you will have to retard the spark.

If you are in a parade and driving in low gear, try to keep the spark well advanced when the engine speed is high. See that the carburetor is properly set and not operating with a rich mixture. If your car overheats only on hard driving and hot days, it is probably not too bad. If it always overheats, the problem will have to be located and serviced.

Thermo-siphon Cooling

The thermo-siphon cooling system has been used on a number of cars. The Ford Model T is a common example. The system operates on the principle that hot water rises and cold water settles. When the water in the block is heated, it rises and passes through the top radiator hose into the top of the radiator. Here it comes in contact with the radiator cooling cores and is cooled by the air drawn through the radiator by the fan. The cooled water passes to the lower radiator tank, up through the bottom radiator hose to the lower part of the cylinder water jackets and the cycle continues.

Make sure that the radiator is clean on the inside and outside. This system has the tendancy to boil. Some of this problem has to do with the design of the cooling tubes. They are round and they do not expose enough surface to the air as do the flat tubes. You might want to have the radiator re-cored, but this will depend on how much of a purist you want to be.

Keep the system clean and watch your driving habits, spark advance and carburetor adjustment and you should make out okay. The temperatures outside aren't much different then they were in Model T days and our roads are a lot better. See that the fan belt is not slipping because it must run the fan fast enough to draw cooling air through the radiator.

You might change the pitch on the fan blades to a sharper angle in order to draw more air through. Accessory water pumps are sold for the Model T if you want to go this route. Keep the radiator full

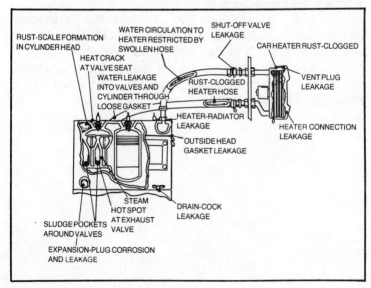

Fig. 8-3. Problems that might occur.

so that there will be a bit of back resistance to force the water forward.

Air Cooling

You already know about the air-cooling system if your weekend companion is the lawnmower. The ducted flywheel draws air in and blows it over the radiating fins, and the air absorbs the excess heat and carries it away. This method of using the flywheel as a blower has also worked very well for the Franklin car. A number of the early cars used an auxiliary blower very similar to the method on the VW and the Corvair. These cars had small bore cylinders and a forced-draft system that circulated air around the cylinders. Problems are few with this system, but accumulated dirt and grease on the engine and the ducting system will hinder the heat flow. Make sure these are clean.

See that the cooling flaps are operating properly and that they are fully open after a hard run. See that the ducts are all in place and that none are missing. If belts are used, check that the cooling fan is free to rotate and that the belt is not glazed and cracked. Tighten as necessary.

Check the ignition timing. If the spark occurs too late, excessive heat build-up and power loss will occur. Check the weight of the oil that you are using. It should be heavier than that used for a liquid cooled engine.

Air-cooled engines have the advantage that in freezing weather they do not have a coolant problem. But they sure do have a heating problem. It is also very difficult to fully control the cylinder temperature with this type of cooling. But an air-cooled engine is less troublesome and simpler in construction than a similar liquid-cooled engine.

Chapter 9
Cooling System Service

The liquid cooling systems usually have a water pump to maintain circulation in the system. The water pump is driven by a belt from the engine crankshaft and circulates the cooling liquid between the radiator and the engine cooling jackets. The cooling liquid is water with antifreeze being added to the water in the winter.

The radiator, which is actually a heat exchanger, is so mounted that it is in contact with the air. The heat is then transferred from the water to the air. The radiator is made up of three main parts: the top tank, the bottom tank and the center core or cooling section. There are several types of radiator cores. Two of the most common types are the tubular and the cellular. The tubular consists of many small tubes placed in rows that run from the top to the bottom tank.

They are held in position by a horizontal series of thin metal strips called fins. These are spaced about one-eighth of an inch apart. The fins help to transfer the heat from the water to the air. As the hot water leaves the top tank and enters the tubes, it is divided into many small streams. As the water is passing through the tubes, it's heat is tranferred to the tubes. This heat is conducted to the fins and carried away by air passing through the radiator core.

The cellular radiator core is made up of a large number of narrow water passages formed by pairs of thin metal ribbons soldered together along their edges and running from the upper to the lower tank. The edges of the water passages, which are soldered together, form the front and back surfaces of the radiator core.

The water passages are separated by air fins of metal ribbon which provide air passages between the water passages. Air moves through these passages, from front to back, absorbing heat from the fins. The fins, in turn, absorb heat from the water moving downward through the water passages and the water is cooled.

An overflow pipe, which serves as an outlet for steam and excess water, is attached to the filler neck on the top tank of the radiator. This pipe leads to the bottom of the radiator where the lower end is left open. A drain cock in the bottom of the lower tank allows draining of the coolant. Some engines have extra drain cocks in the block.

To repair leaks in the radiator core, you must first remove the radiator from the car. Drain the engine and radiator by opening the drain cocks in the radiator and engine block. Then remove the upper and lower radiator hoses. Remove the support bolts, horns, wiring harness and anything else that will interfere with the radiator removal. With these parts out of the way and the radiator loose, lift straight up and out of the radiator support.

If you find leaks in the tanks, they are easy to repair with solder. Use a soldering gun or copper rather than a torch. If there are several leaks in the core, it probably indicates that the core is corroded and might need replacing. Unless you have experience with this type of repair, you will find it better to have the radiator shop solder your old tanks onto a new core.

While you have the radiator out, you should have it properly cleaned if there have been problems with overheating. If you have a particularly old radiator with round tubes in it, you might consider having the core changed to flat tubes. Again, this depends on how much of a purist you are. Cleaning an old core can develop leaks so discuss this with the service man. Sometimes small leaks can be repaired without removing the radiator by pouring certain mixtures into the radiator.

Radiator hoses are used to transfer the coolant between the engine and the radiator. The upper or outlet hose connects the water outlet housing on the top of the engine to the top radiator tank and the lower or inlet hose connects the bottom tank of the radiator to the water pump. These hoses are made of rubber so that they can withstand the vibration between the engine and the radiator.

Some hoses on the lower end have a coil of spring wire fitted inside to prevent the hose from collapsing because of the low pressure produced by the water pump. Hose connections between the radiator and engine might deteriorate and result in leakage or inadequate passage of water. The appearance of the hose and connections will indicate its condition. If the hose is rotted, soft, and collapses easily when squeezed, it should be replaced. To calculate the size of the radiator hose used, measure either the inside diameter of the hose or the outside diameter of the connection. Hose clamps of the spring tension, screw, or worm tightened band type are used to secure the hose to the connection and to prevent leakage.

Engine Fan

When the engine is running, the fan draws air through the radiator core and cools the water in the radiator. The fan can be mounted separately or on the end of the water pump shaft. Some engines are equipped with a fan shroud that improves fan efficiency in that all the air pulled back by the fan must first pass through the radiator. The cooling action of the air caused by the fan is most important while the engine is idling or being operated at slow driving speeds.

A fan belt is necessary to drive the fan. While most belts are made in a V or wedge shape, there are flat belts used also. The wedge belt fits firmly into the pulley grooves so that belt slippage is eliminated by the extra friction. Adjust the flat belt tight enough so that it does not slip. For the V belt, tighten so that when light thumb pressure is applied at a point midway between the drive and one of the driven pulleys the belt will sag approximately its own width (Fig. 9-1).

Inspect the fan blade for small cracks near the center and replace or repair as necessary. See that the blade is balanced and that the pitch on the blades is the same for all before you fasten it to the hub. Check the hub bearings or bushings for wear and replace the shaft or bushings if necessary. If the fan is mounted on the end

Fig. 9-1. Proper fan belt adjustment to prevent water pump and fan slippage.

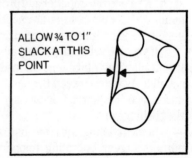

ALLOW ¾ TO 1"
SLACK AT THIS
POINT

of the water pump shaft and the bearings are bad, the pump will have to be repaired or exchanged for a rebuilt one. Check the price of a rebuild kit for the pump against an exchange unit. You will need the use of a hydraulic press to rebuild a pump. Include this in your price.

To circulate water through the cooling system, a water pump is used. The water pump can be mounted at the front end of the cylinder block between the block and the radiator. If it is, then it is driven by a belt connected to the drive pulley attached to the front end of the engine crankshaft.

If the pump is mounted on the side of the block, it can be driven by a gear on the crankshaft or camshaft and a flexible drive. Most water pumps are of the impeller type. They consist of a housing—with water inlet and outlet—and an impeller. An *impeller* is a series of curved blades or vanes attached to one end of a sealed pump shaft. As the impeller rotates, the water between the blades is thrown outward by centrifugal force and forced through the pump outlet into the cylinder block. Cooled water from the bottom of the radiator is drawn into the pump through a hose connected to the water pump inlet. The impeller shaft is supported by one or more bearings and a seal is used to prevent water from leaking out around the bearings. If the pump is noisy or if it leaks, it will have to be repaired. See if a kit is available.

Remove the pump from the car but drain the radiator first. Remove the fan hub or drive pulley with a press or puller. Do not crack the pulley because a new one is not in the rebuild kit. Remove the bearing lock or snap ring. Support the pump body and press out the shaft, bearing and impeller. Examine the pump body sealing surface and if it is free of pits and rust spots you are okay. If not, the pump body must be refaced. This might take a special cutter.

Remove the impeller, but check its position on the shaft first. Replace the seal correctly and remember that it revolves with the shaft. Replace the impeller and press the related parts back into the pump body. Lubricant is not necessary on the seal. Support the impeller end and press on the fan drive or pulley.

If you are rebuilding the type of pump that uses packing, then it will also have bushings instead of bearings and it is easier to rebuild. As before, keep the parts clean and on this style of pump make sure the lubrication passages are lined up before you press the bushings in.

Some cooling systems use a pressure radiator cap which permits higher operating temperatures, increased cooling efficiency and reduced evaporation and surge losses. Water boils at 212 degrees Fahrenheit and atmospheric pressure of 14.7 pounds per square inch. If the air pressure is increased, the boiling point of water is raised about 3 degrees for every pound of pressure added. The water in a system designed to operate under a pressure of 7 pounds would not boil until it reached a temperature of 233 degrees. Because the temperature of the water is above 212 degrees, the difference between air and the water temperature causes the heat to be transferred to the air faster and results in improved cooling efficiency.

The pressure cap fits over the radiator filler tube and seals tightly around the edges. The cap contains the *blowoff valve* and the *vacuum valve.* The blowoff valve consists of a valve held against a valve seat by a calibrated spring. The spring holds the valve closed so that the pressure is produced in the cooling system. If the pressure goes above that designed for the system, the blowoff valve is raised off its seat, relieving the excess pressure.

The vacuum valve is designed to prevent the formation of a vacuum in the cooling system when the engine has been shut off and begins to cool. If a vacuum forms, atmospheric pressure from the outside causes the small vacuum valve to open, admitting air into the radiator. Without a vacuum valve, the pressure within the radiator might drop so low that the outside pressure would collapse it. Check to see that the radiator cap you have is of the proper pressure rating for the cooling system. The pressure rating is stamped on the top of the cap. Check the seal in the cap for tears or cracks and replace the cap if necessary. There are testers that check the radiator cap for pressure and also testers to check the cooling system's ability to hold pressure.

Flushing The Cooling System

The best way to clean the water jackets which are cast into the cylinder blocks and heads is to have them boiled out when you have the engine down for repair. Some models have water distribution tubes that direct water around the exhaust valve seats to prevent "hot spots." These tubes can be replaced during engine overhaul if they are found to be corroded.

Rust clogging is a common cause of cooling system failure. Grease and oil can enter the system through the water pump and cylinder head joint. Coolant circulation keeps loosening the rust as it forms by the chemical action of oxygen and iron. Some of it settles in the water jacket, but the fine particles are carried over into the radiator where they build up a layer of hard scale inside the water tubes.

Lime deposits form scale on the water side of the cylinder barrels and head. The scale, which is a poor conductor of heat, causes overheating. Scale and rust are both caused by the water and the oxygen in the water working chemically on the hot metal. Therefore, preventive maintenance is required to keep the cooling system working. There are safe chemicals on the market which will loosen rust and scale. It's a simple matter to flush the block and radiator clean.

An effective cooling system cleaner should be capable of removing hard rust-scale by dissolving action. Sodium bisulphate and oxalic acid types of cleaners have been found satisfactory. An acid cleaner should preferably be inhibited to reduce cooling system corrosion to the smallest amount possible without affecting cleaning action.

Iron rust and water scale usually build up together in the cooling system. No cleaner has rapid action on water scale, but the acid type cleaners—through their dissolving action on rust—break up and loosen the water scale so that it can be flushed out. Periodic flushing with water will remove loose rust, but flushing is not effective for the removal of hard adherent rust scale or grease.

The use of an acid type cleaner is necessary before flushing to loosen and dissolve the scale. When using such cleaners, be sure to follow the manufacturer's directions to the letter. You will not be able to use a regular garden hose for flushing. You will need an air and water gun. This you can rent or you could decide to have the cooling system flushed commercially. In any event, the procedure is described as follows.

Completely drain the system and put in the recommended amount of acid type cleaner and fill with fresh water. With the radiator covered, run the engine at least 30 minutes after the solution is hot, 180 degrees, but below boiling. Stop the engine and after a few minutes thoroughly drain the system by opening all drain cocks and disconnecting hoses to heaters and other accessories.

Pour the recommended amount of neutralizer into the radiator, fill with water and run the engine until it is warmed up to driving temperature. This will circulate the neutralizer solution throughout the system and completely end all action of any undrained cleaner solution.

Drain the system, fill it with water and run the engine until it is warmed up. Then drain again to complete the flushing operation before the car is driven. Do not leave the neutralizer in the system. It is not a rust inhibitor.

For clogged or overheating systems, double the quantity of cleaning compound and increase the engine running time (depending on the condition of clogging). Flushing with a hose in the radiator filler neck could close the thermostat and prevent thorough flushing of the water jacket. This would leave some cleaning solution in the jacket or car heater that would have a detrimental action on later additions of antifreeze or rust inhibitor.

For the most complete removal of loose rust from the radiator and the water jacket, pressure flushing with an air and water gun is recommended. In case of very severe radiator clogging, the tubes might be so tightly plugged that the cleaning solution cannot reach all the clogging material. Such a condition requires commercial cleaning (Fig. 9-2).

The thermostat is a heat-operated valve that controls the flow of the coolant to the radiator. It maintains the proper engine operating temperature. The thermostat is usually located inside the water outlet housing near the top front section of the engine block or cylinder head. The two types of thermostats used are the bellows and the bimetal spring.

The bellows type contains a liquid that evaporates with increasing temperature. Therefore, the internal pressure causes

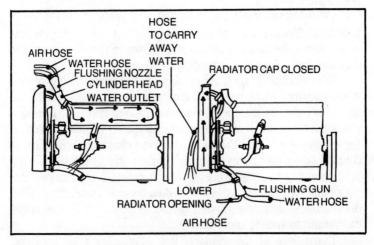

Fig. 9-2. Flush the cooling system in the opposite direction to normal coolant flow. Flush the radiator separately and apply air pressure gradually.

the bellows to expand and raise the valve of its seat. The bimetal spring uses a wax pellet which expands with increasing temperature to open the valve and allow water to circulate between the engine and radiator. The valve will be opened gradually as coolant temperature rises and will reach a wide-open position about 25 degrees above the opening temperature. A thermostat that is marked 180 degrees will be fully open at 202 degrees.

To check a thermostat, suspend it in a pan full of water and heat the water while measuring the water temperature. It should open within 5 degrees of its rated opening and be fully open about 25 degrees above this temperature.

Temperature Gauges

With the higher operating temperatures, it is important that the driver know the temperature in the cooling system. A rise above normal indicates that the engine should be stopped. Warning lights are also used to indicate when the coolant is cold or hot. The two general types of gauges are vapor pressure and electric.

The vapor pressure gauge consists of an indicator bulb and a tube connecting the bulb to the indicator unit. The bulb is placed in the water jacket of the engine and has a liquid in it that evaporates at a low temperature. As the engine temperature increases, the liquid begins to evaporate and create pressure which is transmitted through the tube to the indicating unit. The indicating needle moves across the dial face and the temperature in the water jacket is indicated.

With the electrical gauge, an engine unit is placed in the water jacket and connected to the dash unit by wiring. As the engine unit is heated by the coolant, less current flows in the circuit and the dash unit indicates a higher reading on the scale.

When indicator lights are used, a bimetal engine unit is placed in the coolant. When it is cold, a circuit is completed to the cold indicator light. As the engine warms up, the circuit is broken by a change in the position of the bimetal spring and the light goes off. If the engine overheats, the bimetal spring closes a second set of contacts which completes the circuit to the hot indicator light.

Servicing the vapor pressure unit consists of changing the entire unit. Any break in the tube makes the unit inoperative. With the electrical units, it is a matter of testing the dash unit against the engine unit to find the faulty one.

Regardless of the climate, use permanent type ethylene glycol antifreeze protected to 0° Fahrenheit to help raise the boiling point of the coolant. For winter protection, a mix of one-half water and the balance ethylene glycol will give protection against freezing and the damage of cylinder blocks and heads and radiator cooling system parts.

The lower the temperature the higher the percentage of ethylene glycol in the solution to prevent freezing of the mixture. Use an antifreeze hydrometer to show the freezing point of the solution. If there is not adequate protection, consult an antifreeze chart. Drain the coolant and replace it with the proper amount to ensure cold weather protection.

Service on air-cooled engines should be directed mainly to the belt and the fan. See that the belt is not cracked or glazed and that it does not slip. The fan should be free to rotate when the belt is removed. The ducting must all be in place and securely fastened.

If a cooling problem continues, it might be necessary to remove all the ducting and clean the entire engine of accumulated dirt. Check the oil cooler at this time. If there is evidence of sludge in the engine, the engine should be removed and cleaned. See that you are using the proper weight of engine oil in relation to the outside temperature. Check the valve adjustment and the ignition timing because poor tuning can cause high operating temperatures.

Chapter 10

Drive Line Troubleshooting

The drive line consists of those units that carry the engine power to the rear wheels. They include the clutch and transmission on manual shift cars or the automatic transmission on others, drive shaft and universal joints, differential and rear axles.

Clutch and Transmission

The clutch allows the driver to regulate the engagement of the engine and the drive line to provide smooth starts and also to disconnect the engine without having to shift the transmission in neutral. By means of the transmission, the engine obtains the necessary mechanical advantage over the rear wheels to start the car moving and to keep it moving over different road conditions. It also provides for a reverse gear that permits backing the car up and a neutral position that allows the engine to run while the car remains stationary without having to keep the clutch disengaged.

As you drive your car, you will become more aware of the noises and vibrations that it produces in the various gears. Changes in this noise level might indicate problems in the near future. By careful elimination, you should be able to zero in on the problem before it becomes a major expense.

There is only one service that can be done to the clutch while it is in the car and that is the pedal free-play adjustment. This is the distance the pedal moves before the clutch is engaged. It should be about 1 inch and is set at the clutch linkage. If you find that you cannot maintain the distance, clutch and pressure plate replacement is the only answer. Low clutch life can be the result of poor driving habits or heavy duty use. Do not ride the clutch pedal and do not hold the car on a grade with the clutch; use the brake instead. If you make rapid "gangster" starts, you will get a lot of experience in replacing the clutch and pressure plate. So take it easy (Fig. 10-1).

Listen for noises that you can hear when you move the pedal up and down with the engine not running. The linkage might require lubrication, it might be worn or it might need adjustment. It might also be that the pressure plate lugs are rubbing against the cover assembly.

Start the engine. Keep your foot off the pedal and listen for any local noises. Remember that the shape of the clutch housing will amplify some sounds. Make sure that you know where they are coming from. Press the pedal down just past the free play. If a fairly high pitched noise occurs, then the clutch pilot bearing is at fault.

Continue pressing down on the pedal. If the noise continues, it will be the clutch release bearing because it is in contact with the clutch release fingers. On some models, this bearing can be lubricated. On others it will have to be replaced. If you have too little pedal free-play this could cause the bearing to run all the time and become noisy.

Clutch problems include chattering, dragging, grabbing and slipping. If the clutch chatters while it is being engaged, the trouble is caused by rapid gripping and slipping. These conditions are caused by loose engine mounts, warped or sticking clutch disc, worn linkage or a binding clutch release bearing.

Fig. 10-1. Clutch control showing the threaded rod which will allow 1-inch of free pedal. This is the only adjustment you can make while the clutch is in the car.

Clutch drag means that the clutch disc does not release even though the clutch pedal is fully depressed and gear clash is evident. In most cases, this is caused by excessive clutch pedal free-play. Check this carefully. It's also possible that if the car has not been driven for some time that the disc has seized to the plate or the splines on the clutch shaft.

A slipping clutch is best noticed by a racing engine and very little car movement. If you can start the car in high gear without stalling the engine, you have a slipping clutch. This might be an oil soaked disc caused by a leaking rear main bearing seal or it might be weak springs in the pressure plate itself. Normal disc wear will reduce the clutch pedal free-play and cause slippage because the plate is in the partial released position. Check the pedal free-play.

To determine the cause of noise problems in the transmission, road test the car and check the operation of the transmission in each gear ratio. If the noise is present only during one specific gear ratio, it is probably caused by defective gears pertaining to that respective gear ratio. If the transmission is noisy in each gear ratio, the noise could be caused by improper lubrication, damage bearings, flywheel housing misalignment, loose transmission mounting bolts, or damaged mainshaft or cluster gears.

Check the lubricant for proper level and see that you have the right type of lubricant for your transmission. Drain out some of the old lubricant to see if it is contaminated with metal chips. If you find a gear tooth in the drain plug, don't look around for the tooth fairy. Let the transmission drain right out.

If your transmission has no drain plug, remove the lower bolt on the rear extension housing to drain the transmission. Now remove the side cover. It's a bit easier if you take the shift rods off, but remember what side the washers and springs are on.

If you have a floor shift, take the floorboards out after you have removed. the floor mat. Clean the top of the transmission before you remove the top cover. Use a good trouble lamp and examine the transmission gears. That tooth has to belong to one of them or there has been some pretty slipshod work in the past. If the gears are okay, check the splines and see that the two sliding gears move smoothly. If your car has a synchromesh transmission, which was designed to do away with the clashing and breaking of the gears in the older spur tooth type, have a good look at the unit. *Synchromesh* is the combintion of two words: synchronize and mesh. That is what this unit does. It synchronizes the speed of the clutch shaft with the main shaft by the use of two friction cones. And the two gears mesh quietly. The two speeds that involve this unit are second and third. If you had a noise in those gear ratios, examine the corresponding gears (Fig. 10-2).

If the noise was in first or reverse, examine the sliding gear and the associated gear train for these ratios. The cluster gear is the large gear in the bottom of the transmission case and it should not have any excessive up and down movement.

Be careful if you pry against the gear case with a bar. Examine the reverse idler gear for up and down movement. If noise is only heard when the transmission is in neutral, recheck the cluster gear and the reverse idler for loose bearings and worn teeth. Check the input shaft bearing and the mainshaft bearing.

Remember that you are doing a visual inspection which will decide whether or not the transmission will have to be removed. Check every gear and tooth at least twice. This is not difficult and it is the diagnosis that is important. Replace the drain plug and if the transmission has a top cover fill with proper lubricant to the necessary level and then replace the cover. If you have a side cover, you will have to replace the cover first and then put in the lubricant. Use new gaskets or at least some adhesive on the old one. Don't overfill the transmission. The level should be just at the hole. Road test again and remember that all gear trains have some noise. Don't look for something you can't find.

If your car suffers from a leakage of lubricant, you should correct the problem. Clean the outside of the transmission case and lay a clean newspaper under it. Check for leakage on the paper that might be due to loose bolts, a loose drain, fill plugs or cracks in the transmission case. If the car is of the open drive shaft type, it might have a leaking transmission seal or a worn slip joint.

If you find that the transmission is always low on lubricant and no external leaks show and if the car is of the closed drive shaft type, then the lubricant is leaking out to the differential. This problem should be corrected by new seals or bushings in the torque tube. This condition not only contaminates the oil in the differential, but the brake linings will also become oil soaked because of the high oil level in the differential. Fix this problem before it causes other problems.

If you find that the transmission shifts hard, it might be caused by an improperly adjusted clutch or by the transmission external linkage. Adjust the clutch to have the 1-inch free-play in the clutch pedal. If the transmission has the exterior interlock type linkage, make sure that the cam or wedge parts are not binding and that the interlock is properly adjusted. If the crossover linkage is not adjusted properly or the linkage is bent, there will be a binding or interference condition when you shift from one gear to another.

Disconnect these rods from the shift cover and check to see that there is no binding in the steering column as you move the selector lever. Some cars used a vacuum-assist device that included a vacuum cylinder actuated by vacuum from the engine-intake manifold. When the shift lever movement started, air pressure was applied to one side of the piston and a vacuum was applied to the other side. This difference in pressure caused the piston to move and this movement provided most of the shifting effort. Check all these areas if you experience hard shifting.

If you still have difficulty shifting, then the transmission will have to be removed and overhauled. Just before you start, check all the transmission and flywheel housing bolts for the proper torque. Make sure that the flywheel housing is properly positioned against the engine. Check the torque on the engine rear mounting bolts and the cross member-to-body bolts.

Loose mounting bolts allow misalignment of the transmission in relationship to the torque transfer from the engine to the transmission main drive gear. Misalignment between the flywheel housing and the engine will cause a similar problem. The removal procedures are similar for most transmissions, but the overhaul disassembly might vary. Refer to a shop manual and follow the instructions.

If your car has an automatic transmission, the first test to make is the level and condition of the fluid. Have the lever in Park position with the engine running and the transmission fluid at operating temperature. Pull the transmission dip stick and if the fluid on it is clean and does not smell burned it is okay. The color should be red and the level should be between the ADD and FULL marks.

If the color is brownish to black and the fluid smells burned, it means that a clutch or band has burned out due to overheating. If the fluid is light in color and full of bubbles and the level is high, it means that air is mixing with the fluid causing foaming. A low fluid level will starve the system and cause delay in clutch application. This causes transmission slippage.

A coating of varnish on the dipstick indicates an overheating problem. If you find bits of friction material or metal abrasives on a dipstick, this is a sure sign that the transmission is not going to last long. Most minor problems can be caused by a low fluid level, but if

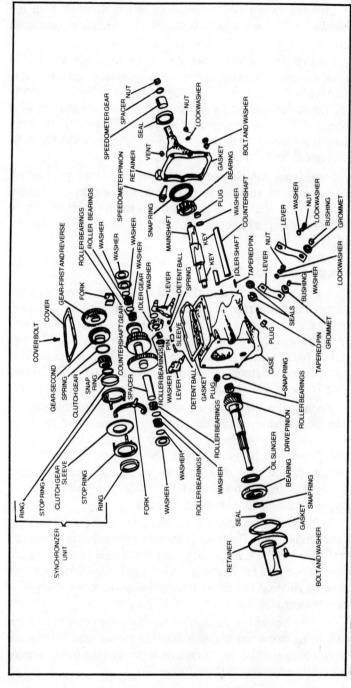

Fig. 10-2. Transmission identification.

this problem cannot be corrected by external repair then the transmission will have to be looked at by an automatic transmission specialist.

Leaks that occur when the car is not moving can be checked by placing a clean newspaper under the transmission and observing where the leakage is from. A leaking pan gasket is best repaired by replacing it, but you can try to tighten the pan bolts and see what happens. If the pan is damaged and leaks, it will have to be removed before you can repair it. The extension housing bolts might be loose and can be tightened.

Some leaks will only occur when the car is moving. You will have to check these after you have taken a test drive. Leakage around the converter housing can show up when a car is not driven regularly and might be repaired by adding special additives to the fluid.

Universal Joints and Drive Shaft

A drive shaft is used to transmit the engine power from the transmission to the rear axle while the universal joint(s) compensate for the change in angle between the drive shaft and the rear axle as the wheels encounter irregularities in the road. The two popular types of drive shafts are the torque tube, or closed drive shaft type, and the Hotchkiss, or open drive shaft type. The former uses only one universal joint, while the latter uses two (Fig. 10-3).

Because the drive shaft transmits torque through the differential to the rear wheels, causing them to rotate and drive the car, a reaction called rear-end torque is developed. This is the tendency of the drive shaft to rotate around the rear axle in the opposite direction to the axle shaft and wheel. To prevent excessive movement of the axle housing, and to attach the housing to the car body, several methods of bracing are used.

In the torque-tube drive shaft, the drive shaft is enclosed in a hollow torque tube. This tube is bolted to the differential housing and attached to the transmission case by a flexible ball type joint. The universal joint is located at the front end of the drive shaft and is free to slide on the drive shaft to compensate for changes in length and angle.

Tubular braces (radius rods) extend from the outer ends of the axle housing to control wheel thrust. The torque tube absorbs the rear-end torque action and transmits it through the transmission, motor, and motor mounts to the frame.

The Hotchkiss drive shaft is a hollow steel tube with a universal joint at each end. The front joint compensates for changes in length while both compensate for changes in the road surface. This type of drive shaft is not designed to absorb any rear-end action. Instead, this action is transferred to the frame through the rear-spring front shackle and the rear springs.

To give flexibility and still transmit power as smoothly as possible, several types of universal joints are used. The most common is the cross and yoke type. The yokes are attached to the driving and driven units and are connected by the center cross. A bearing cup is used in each arm of the cross to help transmit the drive and to permit the yokes to turn freely on the cross. The joint rotates when the driving shaft is at different angles to the driven shaft.

A second type is the ball and trunnion universal joint. The drive shaft has a pin pressed through it. Around both ends is a ball mounted in needle bearings that move in grooves in the outer body of the joint. The body is bolted to a flange on the mating shaft. The rotary motion is carried through the pin and the balls and the drive shaft length is compensated for by having the balls move in the grooves and thereby creating a slip joint.

Other slip joints consist of outside splines on the one shaft and matching internal splines on the mating shaft. The splines cause the two shafts to rotate together and are cut long enough to permit the shaft to change its length without coming out of mesh (Fig. 10-4).

The two most common problems with the drive shaft and the universal joints are noise and vibration. You will notice the first noise when you accelerate the car from a starting position and you hear a loud clunk in the drive shaft. This might be due to loose universal joints. You can recheck by trying the car in reverse and then in forward. If the noise is the same, you might have to replace the noisy universal joint. If you hear a squeaking noise at low speeds and if the joint has a red oxide dust around it, it indicates a

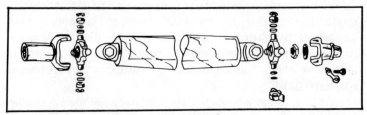

Fig. 10-3. Open drive shaft with universal joints.

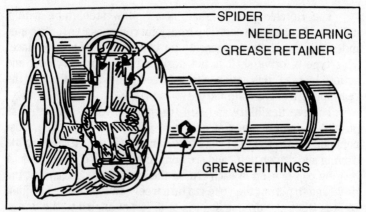

SPIDER
NEEDLE BEARING
GREASE RETAINER
GREASE FITTINGS

Fig. 10-4. Slip joint to compensate for any change in drive shaft length as the rear axles move toward or away from the car frame.

lubrication problem. Some can be lubricated with a grease gun while others will have to be disassembled for lubrication. If the condition continues after lubrication, the joint will have to be replaced.

Vibration at any speed can be caused by a bent, dented or out of balance drive shaft. Worn universal joints or loose clamp bolts will also cause this problem. Remember that wheels, tires, rear axles and the suspension can cause similar noises and conditions. Check things out before you start disassembly. With the covered drive shafts, the universal joint is a bit tougher to get at and it is possible that previous owners have neglected it. But don't just assume that this is the problem.

Differential and Rear Axles

The differential (Fig. 10-5) changes the direction of power from the drive shaft to the rear axle shafts so that the rear wheels can be driven. The speed is reduced and the power is increased by the rear axle gear ratio. This ratio is found by dividing the number of pinion gear teeth into the number of ring gear teeth. However, if the drive shaft is geared rigidly to both rear wheels so that they will rotate together, then one wheel would have to skid when the car was going around a turn. By driving the rear axle shafts through the differential, the outer drive wheel is made to rotate faster than the inner drive wheel. This extends tire life and makes the car easier to control on turns.

As long as there is equal friction between the wheels and the road surface, the axle shafts will turn at the same speed. But if one wheel is put on slippery ice and the other remains on dry ground, then the wheel on the ice will spin at twice the speed it otherwise would while the other wheel remains stationary.

To provide driving torque to the wheel having the greater traction, limited slip differentials have been introduced. To identify a car with the above differential, raise the rear wheels and place the car on stands. Place the transmission in neutral and rotate a rear wheel by hand.

If the axle is of the limited-slip type, the opposite wheel will rotate in the same direction. If the wheel rotates in an opposite direction, the differential is of the standard type. If you decide to start the car while it is on stands, be careful that the addition of your weight doesn't cause one of the rear wheels to contact the floor or ground. You could drive the car off the stands if you put it in gear and the car is equipped with a limited-slip differential.

The rear wheels on cars are mounted on live axles. That means that the axle shaft and the wheel rotate as a unit. There are three types of live axles—semi-floating, three-quarter floating,

Fig. 10-5. Differential.

and full floating. Each type is identified by the manner in which the outer end of the axle is supported in the axle housing.

With the semi-floating type, the wheel end of the axle is supported in the axle housing by a single bearing mounted about 6 inches from the outer end of the axle. The axle must carry the entire weight of the car in addition to transmitting the driving torque. The three-quarter floating axle has the bearing between the outside of the axle housing and the wheel hub. The axle supports only 25 percent of the vehicle's weight. On a full-floating axle, the axle housing carries all the weight and the axle shaft only transmits the driving torque.

The most common rear axle complaint is noise. Excessive noise might indicate a problem that should be looked at before a major problem occurs. However, it must be noted that axle gears make some noise and an absolutely quiet unit is seldom found. When you are evaluating the rear axle, make sure that the noise is not caused by the road surface, by the exhaust system, by the engine, tires, transmission, wheel bearing or by some other external component of the car.

Before a road test of the car is performed, make sure that there is sufficient lubricant of the specified type in the rear axle housing. The level should be even with the filler hole. Drive the car far enough to warm the lubricant to normal operating temperature before testing. A car should be tested for axle noise by being operated in high gear under the following four driving conditions:

Drive. Higher than normal road load power where the speed gradually increases on level road acceleration (15 to 60 miles per hour).

Cruise. Constant speed operation at normal road speeds.

Float. Using only enough throttle to keep the car *from* driving the engine. In float, the car will slow down with very little load on the rear axle gears.

Coast. The throttle is closed and the engine is braking the car. Load is on the coast side of the gear set.

When a rear axle is noisy, the following tests can be made to pinpoint the problem and eliminate the possibility that the noise is of external origin.

Road Noise. Road surfaces such as a rough surfaced concrete or gravel fill on asphalt can cause a noise condition which might be mistaken for tire or rear axle noise. Driving on a smooth asphalt surface will quickly show whether the road surface is the cause of the noise. A road noise usually has the same pitch on Drive or Coast.

Tire Noise. Tire noise can be easily mistaken for rear axle noise even though the noisy tires are located on the front wheels. Sounds and vibrations are caused by unevenly worn tire surfaces or ply separations. Some designs or non-skid treads on low pressure tires, snow tires, and other assorted types cause vibrations.

Temporarily inflate all tires to approximately 40 pounds pressure for *test purposes only*. This will alter any noise caused by tires, but will not affect noise caused by the rear axle. Excessive rear axle noise usually diminishes or ceases during Coast at speeds under 30 mph. However, tire noise continues but with a lower tone as the car speed is reduced. Rear axle noise usually changes when comparing Drive and Coast, but tire noise remains about the same.

Front Wheel Bearing Noise. Loose or rough front wheel bearing noises can be confused with rear axle noise. However, front wheel bearing noise does *not* change when you compare Drive and Coast. Drive the car through a series of left and right turns. This will put a load on the wheel bearings and emphasize a noisy condition if it exists. A light application of the brakes while holding the car speed steady will often cause wheel bearing noise to diminish. This action takes some weight off the bearings. If front wheel bearing noise is suspected, you can easily check it by raising the front wheels and spinning them while feeling and listening for roughness. Also, shake the wheels to determine if the bearings are loose.

Body Noises. The car body or one of the attached components might have a wind noise condition that sounds like a noisy axle. Items such as the grille, radio, antenna, and hood can cause the condition. In some cases, loose body hold-down bolts or brackets are a source of noise.

Rear Axle Noise. Sometimes a noise that seems to originate in the rear axle is actually caused by the engine, exhaust, transmission or power steering. To eliminate the possibility of power steering, fan, alternator or generator bearing noise being mistaken for rear axle noise, drive the car with the belts removed. If the noise does *not* now exist, eliminate the proper component and you are okay. If the noise continues, replace the belts and go on with the tests.

To determine which unit is actually causing the noise, note the approximate car speeds and conditions under which the noise is most pronounced. Stop the car in a quiet place to avoid interfering noises. With the transmission in neutral, run the engine slowly up and down through engine speeds corresponding to the car speed at which the noise was most pronounced. If a similar noise is produced with the car standing still, it is caused by components other than the rear axle or drive line assemblies. If there is no noise, it is reasonably safe to assume that the rear axle or drive line components are at fault. Just to make sure, recheck on a smooth level road.

Noises in the rear axle assembly can be caused by faulty rear wheel bearings, loss of pinion preload, faulty differential or pinion shaft bearings, worn differential side gears and pinions, or by a mismatched improperly adjusted or scored ring and pinion gear set. It is sometimes impossible to determine from a test exactly what internal repairs are required to correct a noisy axle unit. The needed repairs can be best determined by a careful inspection of the wear on the individual parts when the unit is disassembled. Some special tools are needed for assembly, but if you have a service manual for your particular car you can go a long way towards doing the repair yourself.

Chapter 11
Drive Line Service

Before you start the overhaul of any component parts as described in this section, it is wise to obtain a manufacturer's shop manual for details. Check to see that you have the necessary tools to do the job and keep safety utmost in your working procedures.

Clutch Removal And Replacement

Raise the car to a comfortable working height and place it on safety stands. If you are using four stands and your car is of the closed drive shaft type, do not place the rear stands under the axle housing. Place them under the frame and ahead of the housing. The reason for this is that some early cars such as Ford, up to 1948, will have to have the rear axle pushed backward before the transmission can be removed.

If you have only two stands and the car has an open drive shaft, place the stands under the front so that you will have room to move around under the car. Drain the oil out of the transmission and set it aside so that you can examine it later. Disconnect the universal joint (s) and remove the drive shaft.

Keep the universal together by taping it. If you find that the car has floorboards or a floorboard pan, remove it. Check to see if there is a rear transmission mount. If there is, you will have to support the rear of the engine when you remove the transmission. A hydraulic jack does a good job here because you might have to lower the engine to get at the bell housing bolts.

Remove any of the shift levers and disconnect the speedometer cable. Disconnect the parking brake. Remove the bolts that attach the transmission and replace two of them with guide pins. These you can make out of long bolts with the heads cut off and screwdriver slots cut into the ends.

The transmission can be slid back on these pins until the input shaft clears the clutch splines. It is possible to bend the clutch disc if the weight of the transmission sits on the splines. Use guide pins both for removal and installation. On cars with a closed drive shaft, which do not have a means of sliding the torque ball back on the torque tube, the entire rear axle will have to be pushed backward. Disconnect the rear spring U bolts and the shock absorbers. Disconnect the brake hoses or the brake rods and the hand brake cables or rods.

Remove the bolts which hold the universal joint cap to the transmission and disconnect the speedometer cable. Remove the rear wheels and let the rear axle down on the brake drums. See that the rear spring is clear of the rear cross member. If not, the car will have to be raised until the spring clears. Push the rear axle backward until the universal joint disengages from the drive shaft.

Cars that have a sliding torque ball do not require the moving back of the rear axle. Remove the universal joint cap and slide it backward on the torque tube. Support the torque tube and disconnect the universal by splitting it with the bolts. Let the torque tube down and out of the way. Remove the transmission by pulling back and lifting up into the passenger compartment. Use those guide pins and get help if you need it. Some transmissions are heavy.

With the transmission removed, some models will have the clutch completely exposed. On other models, you will have to remove the bottom half of the clutch housing. Disconnect the clutch release fork and remove the clutch release bearing if it didn't come out with the transmission. Use a center punch and mark the clutch and the flywheel so that you will have some identification marks on reassembly. Some units might have been balanced and these marks will insure that the parts will be assembled in the same position.

Almost all clutches used with standard transmissions are similar in construction and operation with the exception of differences in the linkage and the pressure plate assemblies. The clutch assembly is divided into four main parts: the flywheel, the clutch disc, the pressure-plate assembly, and the control pedal and linkage.

A single plate, dry-disc clutch is the mechanical connection between the engine flywheel and the transmission gears. When the driver has his foot off the clutch, the clutch is engaged. This means that the clutch disc is tightly pressed against the flywheel by the clutch plate and the turning effort is being transferred to the

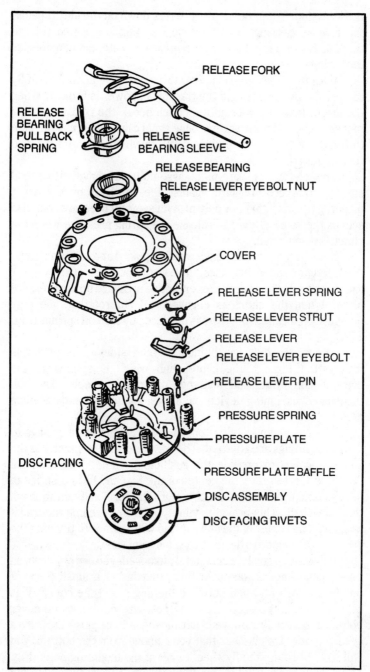

RELEASE FORK

RELEASE BEARING PULL BACK SPRING

RELEASE BEARING SLEEVE

RELEASE BEARING

RELEASE LEVER EYE BOLT NUT

COVER

RELEASE LEVER SPRING

RELEASE LEVER STRUT

RELEASE LEVER

RELEASE LEVER EYE BOLT

RELEASE LEVER PIN

PRESSURE SPRING

PRESSURE PLATE

PRESSURE PLATE BAFFLE

DISC FACING

DISC ASSEMBLY

DISC FACING RIVETS

Fig. 11-1. Pressure plate and clutch disc identification.

transmission. When the driver presses down on the clutch pedal, the release bearing moves forward against the clutch release fingers. Leverage pulls back the pressure plate and compresses the springs.

With this pressure removed, the clutch disc is thrown off by the revolving flywheel and the transfer of power is broken. When the driver takes his foot off the clutch pedal, the release bearing moves back so that the springs once again cause the pressure plate to force the friction disc against the flywheel face and the two revolve together.

The clutch pressure-plate assembly can have either coil springs to exert pressure against the flywheel or a circular diaphragm spring that not only provides spring pressure, but also acts as the release lever to release the spring pressure when the clutch is disengaged.

Some release fingers have weights placed at their outer ends. As the engine speed increases, the centrifugal force on the weights causes the release fingers to exert added pressure on the pressure plate. When the clutch is engaged and not rotating, the only pressure on the pressure plate is produced by the coil springs (Fig. 11-1).

The clutch disc has linings on both sides. The power is transmitted through the center hub which is splined to the transmission front shaft and then on to the wheels. The hub includes a cushioning device and a torsional vibration-dampening unit.

The cushioning device consists of waved cushion springs to which the linings are attached. The waves compress slightly as the clutch engages to provide the cushioning effect. The torsional device is located near the center of the hub and uses a series of heavy coil springs which which absorb the torsional vibrations of the crankshaft. This prevents vibrations from reaching the transmission. The center of the hub is fitted with splines to transmit the power of the engine to the transmission front shaft.

If the clutch cover is completely exposed, you can pry down on the release fingers, one at a time, and insert a small piece of one-fourth inch plywood between the finger and the cover. This releases all the pressure from the pressure plate and the cover bolts can be easily removed. Set these aside because they are a special grade. On clutches that you remove from the bottom, you will have to rotate the flywheel to get at the mounting bolts (Fig. 11-2). Take it easy on the last bolt because the pressure plate and disc are heavy. Release it carefully and don't drop it on yourself.

On the diaphragm-type clutch, you will have to release each bolt a bit at a time as you rotate the flywheel so that you don't warp the pressure plate. When the bolts are about half way out, the pressure is released and they can be turned all the way out. Again, watch your fingers and don't drop the plate and disc.

Examine the disc for signs of oil soaking and determine the cause (engine or transmission) and have it repaired. If you don't, you will be replacing the disc again in very short time. Linings worn down to the rivet heads, cracked and glazed indicate the disc needs replacing. Broken torsion springs or a loose hub indicate the same.

If the disc is good and only the linings need replacement, you might consider making repairs if you can find the material. Check the pressure plate for cracks or grooves and see if the springs are discolored. This indicates a loss of temper and strength. Check the flywheel for similar conditions. If they are obvious, then the flywheel should be resurfaced. To do this, the flywheel must be removed and taken to a machine shop for service.

Before you take the flywheel off, mark its position in relation to the crankshaft and you will be able to put it back to its original position. Examine the ring gear for damage and replace it if

Fig. 11-2. Position marks on clutch cover and flywheel.

necessary. Now is a good time to replace the pilot bearing or bushing. A bad bushing can cause clutch chatter and possible transmission damage. See that the open end of the bearing faces toward the front of the engine. If the flywheel surface has very light heat checks, just break the glaze with some emery cloth so that the clutch disc will seat smoothly.

Do not wash the clutch release bearing in solvent; just wipe it with a cloth. Press the bearing against a flat surface and rotate the outer race while applying pressure to it. It should turn freely without any noise. If not, replace the bearing. Some bearings come with the hub and you will not be able to replace the bearing alone. Coat the inside of this hub with light grease before installation. Bearings that have means for lubrication can be reused if they are not rough or noisy.

If you find that your pressure plate assembly needs rebuilding, do *not* take it apart or you will be visiting your dentist. There is a lot of pressure on those springs and without the proper equipment you're asking for trouble. Try to get an exchange reconditioned one or have your own rebuilt at a shop that does this service.

You should now be ready for reassembly. See that you have repaired any oil leaks from the rear main bearing or the transmission. Replace the flywheel and torque to proper specifications. Put a thin layer of lubrication inside the pilot bushing or bearing race. To align the disc, you can use the input shaft from a similar transmission as a guide.

Make sure the flywheel surface is clean, dry and free from oil or grease. The same goes for the pressure plate (Fig. 11-3). See that your hands are clean. A greasy thumbprint on the flywheel, pressure plate or clutch disc can cause clutch chatter.

Shim the clutch fingers to release the pressure. This will make installation easier. Hold the clutch disc against the flywheel with the correct side facing the pressure plate and pass the aligning shaft through the disc hub and into the pilot bearing.

Start all the fasteners and continue around one turn at a time until the clutch cover is snug against the flywheel. Now use the torque wrench to bring the bolts to proper specifications. Remove the spacers and shaft. Install the clutch release bearing and lightly grease the throw-out fork groove. Lubricate the throw-out fork pivot and install the fork. If an internal retracting spring is used, install it now. See Fig. 11-4.

If the transmission shows any sign of leakage through the input shaft bearing, correct the leak before installation. Wipe the transmission output shaft and see that the splines are clean. Do not lubricate it. Lightly grease the input shaft bearing retainer that supports the clutch release bearing. Use the guide pins to help align and take the weight off the clutch disc. Try to get some help with the transmission or use a suitable hydraulic floor jack.

Place the transmission in gear and slide it on the guide pins. Pass the input shaft and transmission front bearing retainer through the clutch release bearing sleeve. If your transmission is of the style that has the throw-out fork on the transmission, then this part of the job is easier. When the input shaft splines strikes the disc hub, turn the transmission output shaft to align the splines on the input shaft and the splines in the hub.

When the splines are aligned, push the transmission inward and force the shaft through the hub and into the pilot bearing or bushing. Continue pushing the transmission forward until the transmission is seated against the clutch housing. Install the fasteners and bring them to proper torque. Don't use the transmission fasteners to draw the transmission into place. You can keep pressure on the transmission and turn the starter over and see if this will draw the transmission in. If it doesn't, pull the transmission back out and check the alignment of the clutch disc and the pilot bearing.

With the transmission in place, attach the clutch linkage and adjust the clutch pedal free-play. This should be about 1 inch, but check the specifications. Connect the drive shaft. Fill the transmission to the proper level with the necessary lubricant. Before

Fig. 11-3. Couplings.

Fig. 11-4. Clutch cutaway.

you take the car off the stands, check to see that everything is back in place and tightened properly. If you like, you can start the engine and engage the clutch a dozen times or so to seat the disc. Have the garage door open. Now recheck the clutch pedal free-play and readjust if necessary.

Transmission Service

The transmission consists of a number of gears of different sizes which are meshed as required by moving the gear shift lever. There are three forward speeds in the transmission obtained by engaging different sizes of gears in different gear shift positions. There is also a reverse gear. The neutral position provides a means of allowing the engine to run without driving the rear wheels.

In other words, the transmission is nothing more than a mechanical torque multiplier. The gears allow the engine to turn at higher speeds than the drive shaft and at the same time deliver more power. You can start up slowly and smoothly without stalling the engine. Although transmissions vary in construction, most produce a gear ratio of approximately 3 to 1 for low gear and reverse, 2 to 1 for second gear and 1 to 1 for high gear.

Remove the transmission as in the clutch service and wash the outside of the transmission case. Remove the top cover plate or the shifting lever cover if you haven't already done so and check inside the transmission case for bits of metal. If you find particles of brass, this indicates that the synchronizer rings have worn. This can cause rough shifting and also slipping out of second gear. If gear teeth are found, go over each gear very carefully. It is possible to replace only the gears that are broken or chipped if the others are okay.

Wash the inside of the gear case with varsol or solvent (don't use gasoline). Examine the outside of the transmission case for cracks. If cracks are evident, you might consider getting another transmission instead of rebuilding your own.

Use the service manual for your car to help in disassembly. Study the method of construction. This will usually indicate how the parts can be removed. Use a soft hammer to prevent damage and use soft punches when driving the steel shafts. Do not distort the snap rings. Use a pair of snap ring pliers to aid in removal and replacement. Use separate containers for the needle bearings, thrust washers and other small parts. Remove everything from the case and clean all the parts including the case and extension housing. Do a thorough cleaning because a tiny particle of steel can damage an otherwise properly rebuilt transmission.

Examine the input shaft clutch pilot bearing end for wear and scoring. Check the splines for roughness and wearing. Inspect the drive gear for wear, galling, pitting and chipping. Check the condition of the roller bearing contact surface in the end of the shaft.

If the transmission has a synchromesh unit, check the drive gear clutch teeth. They must not have excessive wear or taper as this can cause jumping out of gear. The synchronizer ring contact surface must be true and smooth. Rotate the front bearing and check for roughness and flaking. This bearing must be tight on the shaft with no signs of turning.

Now inspect the output shaft. The bearing surfaces should be smooth. The gears should fit on without excessive play. The splines should be in good shape. Examine every gear; there should be no chipped teeth. If the gear has a synchronizer ring surface, this surface must be smooth.

Examine the countershaft gear or cluster gear teeth. This is a most expensive gear, but if there is damage to it then it will have to be replaced. Check the countershaft and the countershaft bearings for wear. Some bearings are in cage while others are loose needle bearings. Check the thrust washers for signs of wear. Examine the reverse idler gear and shaft for similar wear and check the gear teeth. Some reverse idler gears have a bushing instead of needle bearings. Check the gear on the shaft to determine wear.

Mark the position of the clutch sleeve and the hub on the synchronizer assembly so that they can be reassembled in the same position. Also mark the synchronizer rings and the hub. The rings should have very fine grooves inside and the teeth should be in good shape. The sleeve teeth must also be in good repair and the hub must fit smoothly.

Replace the necessary parts and check the old against the new for size and shape. Use new thrust washers and synchronizer rings to provide the necessary endplay. New gaskets should be used with gasket cement. Lubricate the parts with new transmission oil before installation. Do not use force. If a part will not slide into position, stop and check for the source of difficulty. All moving parts must turn freely without binding. When you are installing the shift cover, align the shifter forks. Install the transmission and make the necessary connections. Fill with recommended lubricant and after a road test recheck the lubricant level.

Work on automatic transmissions should not be attempted without having the manual at hand or you will not get it back together and working properly. You can have the transmission rebuilt at a specialty shop and install it yourself. This is a heavy transmission so use the proper automatic transmission jack—rent if you can. Dropping the transmission could cause physical damage to both you and the transmission.

Universal Joint Service And Drive Shaft

To replace the universal joint on a torque-tube drive, you will have to loosen the rear axle assembly and raise the rear of the car so that you can move the rear axle assembly back. Unbolt the ball retainer from the back of the transmission and push the rear axle back until the drive shaft is free of the universal joint. Unbolt the universal joint from the output shaft and replace as necessary. You might examine the bushings or bearings at this end of the torque tube and any seals that need replacing. The drive shaft is rarely replaced.

Some models do not require the pushing back of the rear axle because they have a torque ball that can be slid back on the torque tube and the universal joint is split at the yokes. The drive shaft is lowered and the rear yoke of the universal joint is taken off the drive shaft. If you find that the torque ball is too tight in the socket to permit easy movement of the rear axle assembly, it can be adjusted by the addition or removal of shims (gaskets) under the ball retainer.

With open drive shaft cars using a slip joint, mark the position of the drive shaft to the slip joint so that the yokes are in the same plane. If the yokes are misaligned on assembly, vibration can result. Raise the back of the car on stands. This will prevent transmission oil from leaking out.

Remove the drive shaft by observing where the flanges or U bolts are located. Do not allow the drive shaft to hang—remove it. You can also tape the rollers in place so that you won't drop them and lose the needle bearings. If you are disassembling the universal joint for lubrication purposes, use a large vise as a press to keep damage at a minimum. Place a large socket against the yoke on one end and a smaller socket at the opposite end on the roller.

Because the vise is closed, the small socket will force the cross to push the opposite roller part of the way into the large socket. When the roller is forced part of the way out, grasp it in the vise and use a soft hammer to stroke the yoke to remove the roller. Do not spill the roller bearings. Force the cross into the opposite direction to remove the other roller. The cross can then be tipped outward and removed.

Wash all of the parts, see if they are free of grooving or chipping, assemble and check for looseness. If any sign of wear is present, replace with a new kit. If the old parts are okay, lubricate with multi-purpose universal joint grease if the bearing is the sealed type. Pack the grease reservoirs carefully to eliminate trapped air. Make sure that each roller has the specified number of needles. The last needle should go in with slight pressure. If it doesn't, then the needles are loose and wear will result. Place the seals over the cross and start the rollers into the cross. Use the vise to squeeze the rollers flush with the yokes. If the snap rings go inside then insert them. If the snap rings go on the outside, use a socket the same size as the roller to bring them down. Make sure that the snap rings are tight against the rollers by supporting the cross and striking the yoke.

With the ball and trunnion universal joints, it is possible to inspect the pin and rollers by first removing the cover and then pushing the body back. Remove the ball and rollers, washers, springs and buttons. Clean all parts and examine for wear. If the pin is tight in the drive shaft do not press it out. This pin, when replaced, has to be pressed into a tolerance of .003 of an inch on both sides. And the pin cannot be replaced by itself; the body must be replaced with it.

The rollers, needles, and centering buttons, if worn, can be easily replaced. If the boot is torn, you will not be able to replace it unless you press out the pin. You might consider shopping for a boot. A boot is not one piece. It has an open side that is closed by bolts. Try some of the rubber adhesives. Because the pin will not come out easily, you must use a press.

Repack the body with universal joint grease on the raceways, but not inside the boot. Lubricate the washers, ball and rollers, buttons, etc. Use a new gasket and place the grease cover in position. Lock by bending the tabs back into place. Install in the car.

Drive shafts having a slip joint might leak oil at the transmission end if the slip joint is of the style that fits on the output shaft splines. Replace the slip joint. If the problem persists, replace the bushing and seal in the transmission extension housing. Some models with automatic transmissions require that the slip joint be greased.

Where U bolts are used, torque as specified. Over tightening will cause shaft shudder and short universal joint life. Where locking tabs are used, bend up one at a time. With the shaft in place, shake it up and down and see if there is any movement. There should not be any movement. Road test. If shaft vibration is present, check for a runout or sprung and badly dented drive shaft. Try to change the yokes by giving them a half turn and then reconnect. This change in phasing might correct the vibration.

Rear Axle Service

Before you start to correct noise problems, consider some of the other common rear axle problems. When the car won't move, a broken axle shaft is a common enough reason. Oil leaking out of the rear drums indicates bearing or seal replacements. Oil leaks at the pinion shaft are the cause of a worn pinion shaft seal or pinion shaft flange. A clunking during each revolution is the sign of a broken tooth. If you keep driving, you are not going to get very far and you certainly won't get back.

If you find that you have lost the drive in one of the rear axles and the tire is right up against the inside of the rear fender, *don't* jump to the conclusion that you have broken the axle.

Some applications of rear axles use an inner end lock (C washer type). If the spacer block or the differential pinion shaft wear, it is possible for the axle ends to move inward and the C washer to come loose and fall out. This will cause the axle shaft to come out of the axle side gears. To repair this problem, raise the back of the frame and support it on stands. Drain the differential housing and remove the inspection plate. Find the C lock and examine it for wear or damage. Push the axle inward as far as it will go and try to slide the C lock into the groove in the axle end.

It should *not* go and if it does then you will have to examine further for wear to see why the axle moved inward far enough so that the C lock dropped out. Remove the spacer and differential pinion shaft. The spacer is available in oversize widths that will prevent the axle from moving too far inward. Check the axle side gears for endplay in the differential case. There should be very little. Too much will cause the C lock to come loose.

To install the C locks, the spacer block and differential shaft are removed. Then push the axle inward as far as it will go. Put the C lock on the axle and push the axle outward. Replace the spacer block and the differential shaft. Axle endplay must be minimal or the C locks will fall out. To change a broken axle or replace an axle on the above type, reverse the above procedure.

To replace axle bearings or seals on this type, first remove the axles and then use a puller to remove the bearing and the seal. Examine the bearing surface on the axle shaft. Replacing the axle bearing and having a poor bearing surface will not solve the noise problem.

On this style of rear axle, if you find that the crown gear or pinion gear need replacing, you will have to remove the drive shaft housing and the differential carrier from the rear axle housing. As before, remove the axle shafts. Disconnect the front universal joint and remove any of the emergency brake linkages. Support the front of the torque tube and let it down with a hydraulic jack.

Unbolt the differential carrier housing from the front face of the axle housing. Now pull the entire assembly forward, support the heavy end and remove it from under the car. You can disassemble this further in the view of making it lighter, but it is better to take it into a shop for service this way.

You have now saved a considerable number of dollars because you don't have to pay labor for this removal. Have a source of new parts lined up so that this assembly can be repaired and you can reinstall it. While you are waiting, check the brake linings and clean-up the necessary parts. Get the proper gaskets and gear oil so that when you start assembly you can finish it.

With other cars that use a closed drive shaft but have a housing that has to be split to service the rear axle, you will have to remove the entire rear assembly from the car. The problem you will have is with the rear spring and there are two ways of handling it.

First, if you use a rear spring expander you can leave the spring on the frame by removing the rear shackles. Examine the shackle pins and bushings for wear and replace as necessary.

The second way is to undo the center bolt while you still have the spring in place. Then undo the rear spring clamps and have the main leaf come out with the rear axle housing. Now it will be easier to undo the main leaf from the housing. When you are assembling, use a long center bolt and the weight of the car to compress the spring.

This style is for Ford, up to 1948, and how much you want to disassemble depends on how much you can do yourself. To replace a broken axle, you will have to disassemble the left side of the housing so that the crown gear will come out. Before this, the brake drums must come off and you should use a puller so that damage is at a minimum.

When you pull the drum off, you will notice that the bearing and seal comes with it. If there has been a problem with grease leaks, etc. examine this area. If the bearing surface on the housing is worn, sleeves are available. Some models have a grease retainer in the housing that is either inboard or outboard. There is also a grease retainer and/or bearing/bushing in the torque tube at the universal joint end. If you find that the differential is constantly over full and leaks at the outer axle ends, check this area.

To replace the axles, unbolt the differential case. These are the same bolts that hold the crown gear. Check all the gears for wear and tooth breakage. Remember that putting in a different axle, whether new or not, will cause a different tooth contact and probably different noise.

How much noise you can put up with depends on you. How many gears you want to replace will depend somewhat on your pocket book; so look before you leap.

When you bolt things up again the axle shaft, endplay should not exceed .010 of an inch. If it does, then there is wear inside the differential case or in the axle side gears. These differentials are not difficult to overhaul, but you will need the proper equipment. If you don't feel comfortable changing axles, then get help on the differential. Check the universal joint for wear before you bolt up.

To remove axles that have the retainers at the wheels, first check to see how the brake drum comes off. Jack up the rear of the car and remove the wheel lug nuts and the wheel. If a large flange is forged to the axle end, the brake drum is held to the flange by small bolts or spring clips. Use a brake adjusting tool or a screwdriver bent to shape and release the brake shoes from the drum.

Clean the drum around the flange. If the drum doesn't come loose, hit the axle end a good sharp blow to free it. Some flanges have an access hole to get at the backing plate fasteners. Remove the nuts from the retainer plate. To keep the backing plate in place, screw a nut back on. To pull the axle, use a slide hammer or a pry bar because the bearing is a tight fit in the housing.

If the axle shaft is broken, you will have to snare the other piece out with a wire. If this doesn't work, you can remove the inspection plate and force the broken piece outward. If there is no inspection plate, remove the other axle and pull the entire carrier housing out. Examine the break carefully and make sure that you have all of the pieces. A very tiny one can create a big problem if it is left in the case.

If you were removing the axle for the purpose of checking the bearing and you find it needs replacement, have this done at a shop because you will need the service of a press. If you are replacing axles, replace the bearing also. The press time alone will pay for a new bearing. If you find the seal needs replacing, use the slide hammer to get the old one out of the housing.

Depending on the method of lubricating the bearing, there will be one or two seals. Drive the new seal in with the lip facing and to the proper depth. Inspect the axle oil seal surface and see that it is smooth. Inspect the splines for any signs of twisting and for wear. Replace any wheel lugs that are stripped or broken.

To remove brake drums that are held to the axle by a taper and key or by splines, you will have to use a puller. Rent one if you want; just be sure it will do the job. This can turn out to be a real afternoon's work, but if you can save the labor on it you will come out ahead.

Other methods include the use of knock-off nuts, heating the hub to expand it, and driving the car with the axle nut loosened off. Don't forget to back off the brake shoes.

When the drum is off, the backing plate must also be removed from the housing end. There will be shims between the plate and the housing so keep them together. Now you will have to use the slide hammer attached to the axle end to remove the axle from the housing.

Examine the bearing for wear, corrosion and cracks. Replace the bearing if you have any doubts. This is press service. Check the seals and replace them if there is any evidence of grease on the brake linings. On cars with tapered roller bearings, the axle shaft endplay is controlled by the shims located between the backing plate and the rear axle housing. General specifications are .008 of an inch.

Center-section service can be performed after both axles are removed from the outer ends of the rear axle housing. The rear universal joint must be disconnected and the drive shaft supported or removed. Where you have a removable carrier you can take it out and have it serviced. When the carrier is part of the rear axle housing, you will have to remove the entire axle out of the car.

You might consider the service of a mobile shop and have the mechanic work on the axle while it is in the car. Regarding doing work on the center-section yourself, I don't think you should attempt it except for replacing the pinion shaft seal or the pinion shaft flange. Don't attempt more than you can handle.

If you find an oil leak at the front of the center-section, wipe everything clean and lay a newspaper under the area. Analyze where the oil is coming from. Are the bolts loose and the gasket not tight? Is the housing cracked? Is the pinion loose in the carrier? Is the flange worn and the seal not holding the oil in?

Replacing the gasket under the inspection plate is not difficult. To replace the gasket under the carrier, you will have to pull the axles. A cracked housing can be welded. If you can move the pinion flange up and down, the carrier will have to be removed and the center-section disassembled and inspected.

If you are loosing oil past the seal, examine that area. First, disconnect the universal joint and move the drive shaft out of the way. See that the rear wheels are free to turn and use an inch/pound torque wrench with the proper socket to measure the pinion shaft bearing preload. Go through several revolutions. Mark the position of the flange to the pinion shaft with a prick punch.

Count the number of threads exposed past the nut and mark the nut position. To remove this retaining nut, you must keep the flange from moving and you need a substantial socket wrench to loosen it. If you don't have the proper tools, don't attempt this service.

When the nut is removed, use a puller to remove the flange. Do *not* pound it off because you will damage the bearings. Examine the flange seal contact surface. It must be smooth and not worn. Examine the splines. If they are worn, the flange should be replaced. If the seal surface can be built up, compare this cost with the cost of a new flange.

Before you pry out the seal, measure the depth to which it is seated. With the seal removed, you might be able to inspect the front pinion bearing and cup. Watch for any shims in this area.

If you are using a leather seal, soak it in light engine oil for 30 minutes to soften it up. Make sure that the seal is the proper size and type. Use a large socket or suitable driver to position the seal. Lubricate the flange and place it in an aligned position. It should go on far enough so that the nut can be started. Do not pound it on because the bearings or ring and pinion gear can be damaged. Tighten the nut and rotate the flange to make sure that the bearings are seated. Keep checking the bearing preload with the inch/pound torque wrench until it is equal to that before disassembly. Check the manufacturer's specifications. Connect the universal joint and fill lubricant level as required.

Chapter 12
Electric System Troubleshooting

It's the annual car rally and everything is going fine. The miles slip by and soon it's time for a lunch break with your friends. You park in a shady spot and join them. Soon it's time to go. You do a walk around, check the levels under the hood, get back into the driver position and engage the cranking motor. Nothing happens; the cranking motor gives a short purr and there you sit. The cranking motor will not crank the engine.

Cranking System Tests

The engine will not start if it cannot be turned fast enough to draw in a full fuel charge, compress it and ignite it. However, good compression is the key to engine performance. An engine with worn piston rings, burned valves, or blown gaskets cannot be made to perform satisfactorily until the mechanical defects are repaired.

Try to turn the engine over by hand. If you have the crank, try it or put the transmission in second gear and rock the car and observe whether the crankshaft pulley turns. If it doesn't, this is probably not an electric problem. There could be coolant in the combustion chamber. Because coolant is noncompressible, the engine will not turn. Maybe the engine has been overhauled and the bearings were set too tight. There could be internal breakage. If the engine will not turn, do not try to start it.

If the engine turns, try the starter again and see if the cranking motor drive was jammed against the teeth of the flywheel. Still nothing? Check the battery. Lay a wet cloth over the cell caps and use a pair of pliers to make a contact between the two posts. There should be a good spark.

Try the lights and the horn. If nothing happens, examine the battery cables. Insert the tip of a screwdriver between the battery post and the cable. If you can crank the engine, the battery cable connections are corroded. Try this at both cables. Remove the cables, clean the cables and the battery posts and reassemble. Check where the ground cable connects to the frame and see that this area is also clean and bright.

If the battery indicates no spark, it is probably discharged. Before you push start, check to see if the generator or alternator belt is tight. You should not be able to turn the pulley drive. If you can, it indicates that the belt is slipping.

If the cranking motor is of the foot-operated type, check where the heavy battery cable enters the switch. Give this a good pull and make sure everything is secure. If the cranking motor uses a solenoid (starting relay) and push button, check the button by using a screwdriver to short across the two terminals.

The solenoid can be checked by holding a pair of pliers so that the handles short across the two large cable terminals. Watch the sparks on this one. If the cranking motor turns during any of these tests, replace the unit that indicates the open circuit. If it doesn't, the cranking motor might have a short in the wiring inside.

If the cranking motor spins without cranking the engine, the drive is broken and the starter should be removed for repairs. If the battery is okay and all the connections are clean and tight—but the cranking motor turns the engine very slowly—it could indicate that the brushes are making a poor contact with the armature.

This could be caused by over oiling of the starter bushing. You should have some idea of the condition of your starter. If it isn't in good shape, you should service it. If you run the battery down because of a poor starter, you will not have a power source for the ignition system. This is very important because the majority of starting problems are caused by defects in the ignition system. The ignition system has two electrical paths. The path operating on battery current and controlled by the ignition switch and the distributor (Fig. 12-1) points is called the primary circuit (Fig. 12-2). The other path carries the high voltage current induced in the coil through the high tension leads to the spark plugs is the secondary circuit. Now, let's assume that the cranking motor is turning the engine over but the engine does not start. See Fig. 12-3.

Ignition System Tests

Locate the distributor cap. It might have four, six, eight or more high-tension leads extending from it to the spark plugs. Pull the center lead out of the cap. This should be the one that leads to the coil. The coil is the step-up transformer that increases the battery voltage so that it can jump the spark plug gap. Holds this wire about one-fourth of an inch away from the engine block and crank the engine over.

This might be a good time to enlist some help from your passengers. The test is not impossible to do by yourself, but a little help is convenient. Switch the ignition on. If there is a thick blue spark jumping this one-fourth inch gap, you have isolated the problem to the secondary circuit. If there is no spark, the problem is in the primary circuit and you must repair it first.

Remove the distributor cap from the distributor body by releasing the spring clips. Don't pull out any of the remaining high tension leads. Leave them in the cap. You should now be looking at a black piece of material with a spring clip attached to it. This is the rotor and you can remove it by pulling upward on it. You will now be able to see the points and related parts.

Turn the crankshaft until the contact points close. Now use a screwdriver to open and close the points with the ignition switch *on*. With the high tension coil wire held as before, a good spark should jump to ground. This indicates that the primary circuit is okay. Now try the same test using the cranking motor. If no spark occurs, check the point setting by turning the crankshaft until the

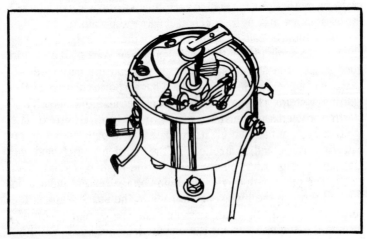

Fig. 12-1. Distributor.

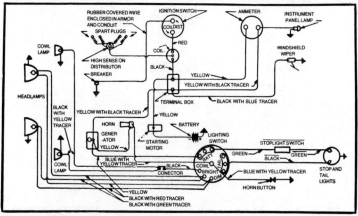

Fig. 12-2. Model A wiring diagram.

rubbing block on the point set is on the high part of the cam. The points must be open at least the thickness of the cover on a penny match pack. If the cam does not turn when the crankshaft does, the problem is in the distributor drive. This is a mechanical problem and not an electrical problem.

If the cam turns and the points open and close okay, but no spark occurs, place the blade of the screwdriver against the movable point and make intermittent contact against the contact point base plate with the tip of the screwdriver. Contact points open. If you get a spark at the high tension lead, the points are defective. The majority of ignition problems are caused by faulty contact points. Check this area very carefully. If you still get no spark, the problem could be a defective coil or condenser.

The condenser is that little cylindrical can either inside or outside the distributor housing (Fig. 12-4). It generally causes very few problems although it can short out and ground the primary circuit. The condenser should be checked with proper test equipment, but the following technique can be used to isolate the problem. Remove the screw that attaches the condenser to the contact base plate or the distributor housing.

Place the condenser so that no part of the metallic can touches the distributor. Insulate the points with a penny match cover between them. Use the screwdriver to make contact between the movable point and ground which is the contact base plate. You should get a low tension spark. This indicates that the primary circuit is complete. Reconnect the condenser. If you do not get any spark, the condenser is shorting to ground and should be replaced.

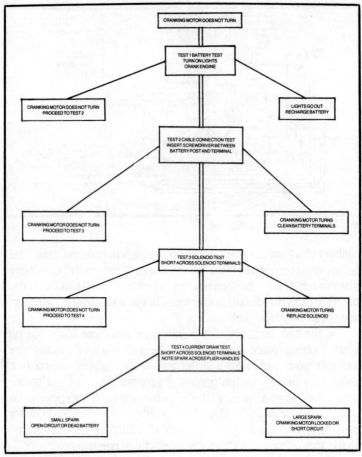

Fig. 12-3. Cranking system tests.

If there is no spark with the condenser out, trace back along the primary circuit to find the defective unit which is open or shorted to ground. Use a jumper wire and short each unit to ground. The defective unit will be the one in which you get a low tension spark at one of its terminals and no spark at the other. Check the ignition switch, the primary side of the coil and the primary wire of the distributor. If the condenser and primary wires are okay, but the engine still doesn't want to start, the trouble could be in the secondary circuit.

With the coil discharging spark, the problem can be at the rotor, distributor cap, high tension leads or spark plugs. If no spark occurs at the high tension lead, the coil or the lead is at fault.

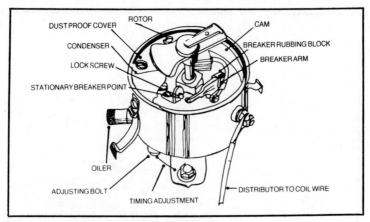

Fig. 12-4. Distributor identification.

Examine the rotor for cracks and replace it on the distributor shaft. Hold the coil wire about one-fourth inch from the rotor spring and crank the engine with the ignition on. If a spark jumps to the rotor, it is shorted to ground and should be replaced. If no spark jumps then the insulation is good.

Examine the inside of the distributor cap for cracks, powder burns and missing carbon tip. If any of these problems are present, the cap should be replaced. Pull one high-tension lead at a time from the cap and examine for corrosion. Scrape the cap and the wire.

Unless you can see the spark escaping on the outside of the plug to ground, which would indicate faulty plugs, check for spark coming to each of the spark plugs. Do this by holding the spark plug lead away from the spark plug and cranking the engine. There should be good spark at each plug terminal.

Now check the plugs, one at a time, by removing them from the head and connecting the spark plug cables and grounding the spark plug case. Crank the engine with the ignition *on*. If there is no spark at the plug, the plug is at fault. It's unlikely that all the plugs and all the spark plug cables would fail at one time. If you think that the tests indicate this, you had better start over again at the distributor cap. See Fig. 12-5.

Charging System Tests

The purpose of the charging system is to keep the battery at full charge and to provide current for the lights and other accessories. The generator, which provides the electricity, might

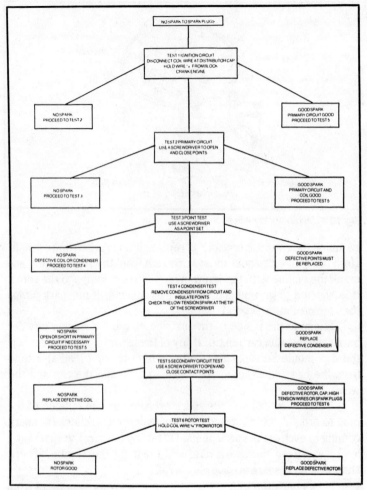

Fig. 12-5. Ignition system tests.

be the two-brush type with external regulation or the three-brush type with internal control.

Somewhere on the instrument panel there will be an ammeter or a generator light that indicates what the charging system is doing. The ammeter will usually show a high charging rate for a few minutes after the engine has been cranked and then drop to five amps or so at highways speeds. At idle, the ammeter will indicate a low charge. However, if many accessories are being used it might show a discharge.

Let's go back to the problem of cranking motor not cranking the engine. If you have been driving with the generator light on or the ammeter showing constant discharge, there has been no charging taking place at all. You have a dead battery. If you have noticed a high temperature reading on the heat gauge, it is possible that the fan belt is broken or slipping. If the belt is in one piece and properly tensioned, then the problem is electrical.

Check the battery. Depending on its location and method of hold-down, see whether the case has cracked and if you have lost all the electrolyte. Check the electrolyte level. It should at least cover the top of the plates. It's possible that the battery in the car is of low capacity and that you are drawing out more than you can put back in. The result is that the battery is always in a discharged condition. The battery might also have a defective cell which would warrant battery replacement.

Check all the connections and see that they are bright and tight. Check the battery connections on both ends of both cables, terminals on the generator, terminals on the voltage regulator or cutout, terminals on the back of the ammeter and the ignition switch, and terminals on the coil and distributor. Use a knife or an emery board to brighten all the connections and then tighten them.

If your car has a three-brush generator with a cutout mounted on the top of the generator, remove the inspection band and look inside. If you find a thin ring of solder on the inside of the band, it means that the generator has run hot. If you can smell burnt varnish and such, you can be sure that is has been running hot and the problem is the generator.

Check to see if the brushes are free to slide in the brush holders and that the springs are not broken or out of place. The *commutator* is the end the brushes rub against and it should be clean and smooth. If you oiled the generator before the rally and got oil over the commutator, this might be the reason it is not charging. Slip the cover off the cutout. The points should be in the open position. If the points are pitted or dirty, use the striker on a penny match pack to clean them up.

Start the car either by crank or with a booster battery and observe the ammeter. If it charges fine. If it doesn't charge, press down on the brushes with the point of a screwdriver and watch the ammeter. If it charges now, it means that the brushes are not making proper contact with the commutator. This could be due to worn brushes. You could stuff some paper between the spring arm and the brush to increase the pressure and probably get home.

With the engine running, use the screwdriver to short out the generator terminal to the case and see if you get any spark. A spark would indicate that the generator is working. With the engine running at better than idle speed, the points in the cutout should close. If they don't and the generator does indicate charge at the terminal, the cutout needs replacing. If you decide to use a manual method of closing the points and the ammeter does indicate charge, don't forget to open the points when you shut the car off or the battery will discharge through the generator.

With the two-brush generator, you can make similar tests except to check for generator output. For this test, use a screwdriver and ground the generator field (F) terminal and observe the ammeter. If it charges full-gauge reading, it means that the regulator is inoperative. On some model generators, you will have to use the screwdriver between the field (F) terminal and the armature (A) terminal to check for generator output.

During this test, don't bring the engine speed to high because you are running an uncontrolled generator. Turn off all the accessories so that they won't be damaged. With this test, you will be able to analyze whether the regulator is working. If you find that it isn't working and all the wires to it are bright and tight, remove the cover and check the points for pitting and oxidation.

You might try cleaning them. However, it is doubtful that without proper adjustment that you will get it to work. Its much cheaper to just buy an exchange rebuilt regulator and put it on as per manufacturer's instructions. You will not be able to go anywhere with a dead battery and if the charging system is not working you will not have ignition. Have the battery charged so that you can continue.

Lights And Accessories

The frame and other metal parts of a car are used as a common conductor for the return of the current to the source of supply. When this current decides to take a "short" cut back to the source, thereby bypassing the load, you have what is commonly called a *short circuit*. A *fuse* is a very fine wire that is connected to the circuit. If the load is exceeded, the fuse wire melts and the circuit becomes broken or open.

Some cars use *circuit breakers* instead of fuses. The advantage is that the breaker opens when the current passing through it exceeds the rated level. The breaker then closes automatically after a period of time or when the current drops to its rated capacity. Newer cars are now using *fusible links* which are short lengths of smaller gauge wire spliced into the circuit. If the circuit is overloaded, the fusible link melts first and prevents the wiring harness from being burnt and the car going up in smoke.

Locate the fuse panel in your car. It is usually on the firewall or forward of the dash. Check the ampere rating of the circuits. It's a good idea to have some spare fuses for emergency purposes. If you blow a fuse, it is possible that the circuit was momentarily overloaded. You could replace it with no further problem.

However, if you blow the second fuse you better look around for the cause of it. The most common cause is a wire with poor insulation that shorts out against the metal car parts. A piece of tape will fix it up and when you get home you can replace the wire.

If you find that the headlamps are getting dimmer as you drive along—and you know the battery is okay—the generator is indicating charge, you have trouble with the lighting circuit. Cars that use light bulbs in the headlamps might show this problem sooner, but it can also happen to sealed units.

Remember what I said about the ground circuit; it must be complete so that the current can get to the ground terminal of the battery.

Start again and make sure that the battery ground strap is bright and tight and that its contact point on the frame or block is the same. If you have a length of wire, run it from the bulb socket to the frame and see what happens. If the light becomes brighter, the problem is a poor ground due to poor contact between the socket and the holder, or the holder and the fender, or the fender and the body. Troubleshoot the other headlamp the same way. If a similar problem exists at the parking lights or taillights, fix them also. For sealed unit, trace back the ground wire and use a jumper to the frame (Fig. 12-6).

If you find that there are no lights at all, you probably have a bad switch. But make sure that you have good contact at the terminals. The dimmer switch could cause a similar problem. The brake light switch might be stuck and cause the brake light to stay on. If this is a mechanical switch, you might be able to free it. If the switch is hydraulic, replace it. In regards to heater switches and electric windshield switches, they are probably not serviceable and the only solution is to replace them.

To replace a sealed headlamp unit, first eliminate the bad lamp by using the dimmer switch to see which beam is out. The burnt lamp is usually darker than the rest, but check it out. If you notice a

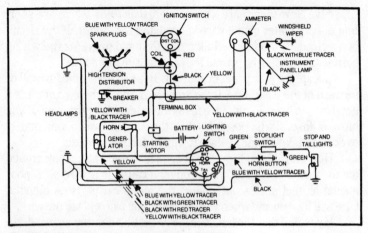

Fig. 12-6. Wiring diagram for an early Ford Model A.

rock through the lens, it shouldn't be difficult to decide which headlamp needs replacing.

First, remove the chrome ring or the decorative trim that surrounds the headlamp. Do you see the retaining ring that holds the headlamp in place? There are three screws that you need to loosen so that you can twist the ring slightly and remove it. Those other two screws are for headlight adjustment; do not move them. Now pull the headlamp off the plug. replace with a good headlamp and position the word TOP in its proper place. Replace the retaining ring and the trim.

To replace bulbs in the taillights, parking lights, etc. remove the trim ring and the lens. To remove the bulb, give it a twist and pull out. Check the bulb by seeing if the filament(s) are in one piece. Giving the glass a tap with your finger will usually get the filament to vibrate and you can tell whether the filament is broken or not. If the bulb is good, check the wire in the socket for current. If everything is okay, the socket and bulb are oxidized. Clean everything up and try it. If you still have no light, try a wire to a good ground on the frame.

Although not specifically known as accessories, there are a number of indicating devices on the instrument panel of a car. These might include the fuel level, oil pressure, temperature and ammeter gauges. Some of the above are indicator lights only. There is also a high-beam indicator lamp and a turn signal indicator. To replace the bulbs for these, you must get in behind the dashboard. To check the gauges, a known good gauge can be substituted for the one causing problems.

Chapter 13

Electrical System Service

Some of the tests and work done on the electric system takes specialized equipment. There should be no need to own such equipment. Other tools *are* necessary for preventative maintenance. Don't buy any tools or equipment if you are not going to use them. Consider the cost of having the service done over the cost of having equipment around that is rarely used. Do only those service procedures that you are comfortable with and understand.

Battery Service

The battery is the most important part of the electrical system and it does not store electrical energy. The energy stored is chemical energy. It is transformed into electric energy when a circuit is completed across the terminals of the battery. When an external current from either a battery charger or a generator is applied in the proper direction to the battery, the chemical process is reversed and the battery is once again capable of producing electric energy. This charging and discharging process continues until the battery chemicals have no more useful life. To extend the service life of the battery, periodic inspection and maintenance is required.

Observe the following safety rules when you are working on batteries.

●If the electrolyte comes in contact with your skin or eyes, flush with cold water.

●Neutralize clothing with a mixture of baking soda and water after a cold water flush.

●Keep sparks and open flames away from batteries. An explosion could occur.

- Use a proper fitted carrier to move batteries.
- Store charged batteries in a cool, dry area.

Locate the battery and give it a visual inspection. Examine for signs of corrosion, cracking and leakage, frayed or broken cables, loose hold down, dirty top, and the level of electrolyte.

Remove the battery cables. Use a battery cable puller to prevent damage to the case. Cover the vent holes with masking tape and brush a solution of baking soda and water over the terminals, posts, and battery top. Let the solution work until the foaming stops. Apply fresh solution where needed. Rinse with clean water. Wipe dry. Brighten the posts and cables and replace cable ends if they are corroded thin. Tighten securely. Remove masking tape. Replace the hold-down if it has been corroded out. Use grease on the hold-down bolts and nuts and the top of the cables and posts to prevent corrosion. Remove the cell caps and see if the electrolyte is above the top of the plates.

You need a hydrometer. Buy one that has a thermometer built into it. This measuring instrument is an accurate way of determining the condition of the battery. The electrolyte (mixture of water and sulphuric acid) is drawn into the barrel where its density is measured by a calibrated float (Fig. 13-1). The higher the reading, the higher the state of the charge of the battery. Make the correction for temperature. Four points must be subtracted or added for every 10 degrees below or above 80 F.

A fully charged cell will test between 1.265 and 1.290.

A three-quarters charged cell will test between 1.250 and 1.265.

A one-half charged cell will test between 1.225 and 1.250.

A one-quarter charged cell will test between 1.200 and 1.225.

Any reading below 1.225 and the battery should be given a recharge. This can be done at home with a "trickle" charger instead of paying the service station. Test the cells during charging to tell when the process is complete. The charging rate should not exceed six amperes and the length of charging time should not be more than 48 hours. The reading should not be less than 1.265 on the hydrometer. If any cell is lower than the others by .050 or more, the battery's useful days are coming to an end.

If you find that a longer charge time is needed, the battery is highly sulphated and the charge rate should be reduced. Excessive electrolyte temperature is another sign that the battery is sulphated. A sulphated battery is one in which the active plate materials harden and resist the essential chemical reactions that are necessary for proper battery operation.

Check the electrolyte level before charging and fill as necessary. Use pure tap water or save defrosting water in a glass container. If you find that the electrolyte level is always low in the car battery, this is caused by overcharging. The excessive charging heats up the battery and evaporates the water. Have the voltage regulator checked at a service shop before more serious problems develop.

Attach the charger Postive lead to the battery Positive post and the Negative lead to the Negative post. The vent caps may remain on, but see that the vent hole is open. As charging progresses gassing will develop. This gas is highly explosive and can be set off by a spark from the battery charger. Shut the charger

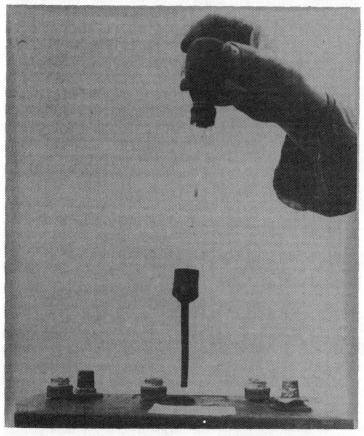

Fig. 13-1. Determining battery condition by the use of a hydrometer.

off before removing the clips from the battery posts. Smoking is also a bad sign. The battery can explode and scatter the case and the acid. Believe it!

There are battery tests for load and no load, but they can only be made accurately when the battery is up to full charge. Special test equipment is required. If the hydrometer reading shows a poor battery, what makes you think other test equipment would indicate something different?

Cranking Motors

The cranking motor circuit consists of the battery, cranking motor, cranking motor drive, control switch and the wiring to connect these units. The cranking motor converts electrical energy into mechanical energy to crank the engine for starting purposes. The cranking motor drive connects the cranking motor to the flywheel ring gear. The two types of drive assemblies in common use are the Bendix drive (Fig. 13-2) and the overrunning clutch drive.

On the early cars, these drives were engaged manually. Later, electrical control switches were used with either the magnetic switch for the Bendix drives or the solenoid control for the overrunning clutch drives. Both were operated by a separate dash switch which was later incorporated as part of the ignition switch. The large amount of current used to operate the cranking motor requires that the cables be large enough and that all the connections be clean and tight to carry the current without undo resistance or voltage drop.

Before you remove the starter from the engine, disconnect the battery ground strap and then the cables and wires from the starter. Use masking tape to identify where the wires go. Undo the bolts that hold the starter to the flywheel housing. On some models, these will be the long bolts that also hold the starter together. View the ring gear and turn the engine over by the front pulley or by prying on the ring gear with a large screwdriver.

If the ring gear is stripped or broken, it will have to be replaced. This means that the flywheel has to come off and you can decide whether you want to pull the engine or the transmission to get at it. This is a service that you can do yourself and save some money. It will take time, but before you start make sure that you can get a new ring gear. Sometimes you can move the ring gear around on the flywheel to expose different teeth.

Examine the starter and decide what repair work you are going to do. If the starter motor ran, but failed to crank the engine, the problem lies in the drive assembly. This assumes that the ring gear is all right. Check for a cracked spring on the Bendix drive. This is usually caused by backfire during cranking. After the drive is repaired, check the ignition timing. You might not be able to buy only parts for the repair of this drive. If you have another one around, see if you can make one good one out of two. The drive should be clean or the gear will not slide on the screw freely. Wash it in solvent and wipe with an oily rag.

Cranking motors with the overrunning clutch should not be washed. They are packed at the factory and cannot be lubricated in service. The gear should turn clockwise, but not in the opposite direction. See that the bushings inside the assembly slide on the shaft freely. Clean the shaft if necessary. There are no parts available for this drive. It must be replaced as a complete unit. Check the bushing in the end of the case. If it is worn, the armature will drag on the field coils inside the case. Before you put the

Fig. 13-2. A Bendix starter drive.

starter back, hook it up to a battery and see that it turns freely and at a fairly high speed. Secure the case when you do this test to prevent an accident.

If you find that the speed is low, it is possible that the bushings are poor, the shaft is bent or there is a bad armature or field coils. With these problems, the cranking motor will have to be taken apart and inspected. Mark the position of the endplate to the field frame to ensure proper assembly.

The brushes might be located either in the endplate or the field frame. Take care and pull the springs back so that the brushes will be free. If the brushes are held with screws and come with the endplates, then remove the springs and the brushes from the endplate. Clean all the parts but do not wash the armature or field coils in solvent; wipe them with a clean cloth. Examine the parts for wear. The brushes should be replaced if they are worn to half of their original length or about five-sixteenth of an inch. If they are worn, they will allow the starter to drag.

The commutator should be smooth. If it is dirty, it can be cleaned with very fine sandpaper. If it is worn or rough, it should be turned down in a lathe. The field windings should have good insulation and not touch the case.

If all the cranking motor needs is a good cleaning and a set of new brushes or bushings, then do it. However, if you found that the cranking motor didn't rotate too well, and when it was disassembled it was found to be in very poor shape, then it is more economical to exchange it for a rebuilt unit than it would be to put new parts into it (Fig. 13-3).

Before you start putting in new bushings and brushes, take the commutator, the field frame with the windings in it and the endplate to an electrical shop and have them tested. If the commutator is rough, it will have to be turned down and possibly undercut. Check the bearing surfaces. If they are very much undersize, they should be trued up and you will have to get bushings to match. If this can't be done, then the armature will have to be replaced.

To replace the bushing in the endplate, either drive it out or use a small slide hammer to pull it out. You could also use a chisel or even a hacksaw blade to weaken the bushing enough so that it can be removed. See that the bore is smooth and press a new bushing into the proper depth.

If the bushing uses an oil wick hole, drill the bushing after it is in place. Remove the burrs and clean out the hole. Use the proper

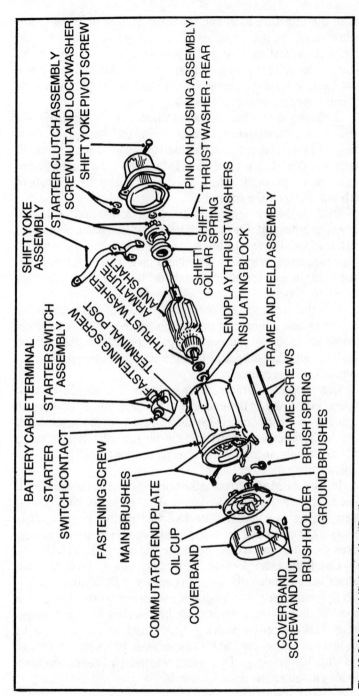

BATTERY CABLE TERMINAL

STARTER SWITCH CONTACT

FASTENING SCREW

MAIN BRUSHES

COMMUTATOR END PLATE

OIL CUP

COVER BAND

COVER BAND SCREW AND NUT

BRUSH HOLDER

GROUND BRUSHES

STARTER SWITCH ASSEMBLY

FASTENING SCREW

TERMINAL POST

THRUST WASHER

ARMATURE AND SHAFT

SHIFT YOKE ASSEMBLY

STARTER CLUTCH ASSEMBLY

SCREW NUT AND LOCKWASHER

SHIFT YOKE PIVOT SCREW

PINION HOUSING ASSEMBLY

THRUST WASHER - REAR

SHIFT SPRING

SHIFT COLLAR

ENDPLAY THRUST WASHERS

INSULATING BLOCK

FRAME AND FIELD ASSEMBLY

FRAME SCREWS

BRUSH SPRING

Fig. 13-3. Manual shift starter identification.

141

end of the armature shaft and try it for fit. These bearings are prelubricated or the absorbent bronze type and do not need additional lubrication. Just add a drop or two on the assembly. Replace the drive housing bushing in a similar fashion. Some cranking motors use a center bushing and the fit here is not as critical as the endplate or drive housing bushing.

Replace the brushes as a set so that wear is equalized. On some motors, the brushes are soldered. See that you place the new brushes in the same position and use rosin core solder. Wash off any excess flux. Brushes that are held by screw must also be placed on the brush arms in the proper direction. Usually the long side of the brush is toward the armature.

Replace the springs if they are weak or distorted and show signs of overheating. Check the brushes for free movement in the brush holders. To seat the brushes to the commutator, use a strip of fine sandpaper wrapped around the commutator (grit facing out) brushes in place on the endplate and sand the brushes in. Blow out all the fine particles.

Pull the brush springs back enough so that the brushes are clear and place the springs beside the brush to hold it in place. Sometimes it seems you need six pair of hands to get this end together, but don't despair. Place the armature through the field frame and into the endplate.

Don't forget the thrust washer if one is used. Check your aligning marks and fit the endplate to the field frame. Don't pinch any wires or brush leads. Depending on the type of starter drive, slide the drive housing on and start the through bolts. If the through bolts don't tighten to the starter end, use two nuts to hold this cranking motor together.

Use a hooked wire to place the brush springs on the brushes. If some brushes are not screwed on to the field leads, do it now. A screw starter is a handy little tool to have for this job. It is necessary to check pinion clearance on some types of overrunning drives. See the manufacturer's specifications for your model.

Check the control switch. If it is the manual type, see that contact is made when the switch is engaged. Polish the contacts with fine sandpaper. The magnetic switch can be checked on the car while the solenoid switch can be checked on the cranking motor. Test the starter before you put it back on the car. Give it a free test run and tap the cranking motor ends with a soft hammer to help align the bearings. To prevent overheating, never operate a cranking motor longer than 30 seconds.

When installing, clean the mounting flange so that the cranking motor will have a good ground connection and check that the starter is in good alignment with the opening. Connect wiring and the ground strap. If you still haven't serviced the battery, why not do so now.

Generator Service

The charging circuit consists of either a generator or an alternator which converts mechanical energy into electrical energy. A regulator or a third brush regulates the amount of current being produced in relation with the amount being used and the state of the charge of the battery. The battery stabilizes the entire circuit. An ammeter or indicating light lets the driver know what is happening.

If there is no output from the generator, you will have to remove it for service. Identify the wires before you remove them. The smaller wire is usually field (F) and the larger wire is usually the armature (A). Loosen the necessary bolts and the slotted adjustment bracket and remove the generator from the engine.

Undo the two through bolts that hold the brush endplate and pull the generator apart. If the brushes are worn down or sticking in the holders or the end of the commutator is greasy, you have found the cause of a no-charge situation. Do not wash the armature or field coils; wipe them clean. If the commutator is not burned or pitted, you can use some fine sandpaper (#00) and clean it up.

The brushes can be replaced and sanded to shape by drawing a strip of fine sandpaper under them after they are positioned against the commutator. If the endplate uses a bushing and needs replacing press, pull it out and replace it with a new one. If an oil wick is used, drill the bushing as necessary. Some generators use ball bearings in both the drive and brush endplates.

If these bearings are of the serviceable type, wash them out and inspect for roughness. Pack them with grease and replace. Bearings that are sealed are of the nonserviceable type and will have to be replaced. To service or replace the bearing in the drive end, you will have to remove the fan pulley nut. To do this, put the belt in the fan pulley groove and tighten it up so that you can loosen the fan pulley nut. You can also hold the armature in the vise, but do not hold the fan pulley because you will damage it.

Now you can remove the fan pulley and the key that holds it to the shaft. To remove the drive endplate, use a press or replace the pulley nut until it is flush with the shaft. Use a soft hammer to tap the shaft down. Examine the bearing surface on the armature shaft. If there are signs of the bearing turning on it, instead of with it, the armature will have to be replaced. Make the same inspection on the endplates. The bearings must fit tight or the endplates will have to be replaced (Fig. 13-4).

Before you replace any bearings, bushings or brushes, examine the armature and field coils for signs of overheating. One good sign is a ring of solder on the inside of the inspection band (if your generator is so equipped). Check for burned commutator bars. This might indicate an internal electrical problem. Take the armature (but don't take out field coils) and the brush endplate to an electrical shop and have them checked.

If you find that one of these components is unsound, balance the price of an exchange generator over the cost of repairing the one you have. If the armature tests okay, have it recut and polished as necessary. Reassemble and replace the parts as mentioned earlier. The fan pulley should spin freely, smoothly and quietly.

To check the generator before installing it on the car, make it run as a motor. Do this as a bench test by using the car battery and a set of battery cables or a set of booster cables. Connect the ground end of the battery to the generator frame. This would be the same post as the cable that attaches to the frame of the car. Connect the other battery post to the armature (A) terminal of the generator. Depending on the type of generator, use a jumper wire to connect either the field (F) terminal to the armature (A) terminal or use the jumper wire to ground the field (F) terminal to the generator frame. The generator should now run as an electric motor.

Install the generator so that the pulley is aligned. The fan belt should be in good condition (no cracks or glazing). Adjust the tension and tighten all the generator connections. Do *not* start the engine. The generator must first be polarized. This means that the current must flow through the field windings in the proper direction. For generators manufactured by Prestolite or Delco-Remy, hold one end of a jumper wire against the regulator BAT terminal and scratch the other end on the regulator ARM or GEN terminal. For generators used on Ford products, remove both the regulator BAT and FIELD leads. Scratch the two wires together and then replace.

Start the engine and watch the ammeter or charging light. The charging light should be out and not a glowing red. The ammeter should read on the high end of the scale for a short time and then return to a reading of a few amperes. If this is not happening and the fan belt is properly adjusted, check the generator for output to be sure that it is working properly. Use the jumper wire between the field (F) terminal and ground or armature (A) depending on the type of generator.

There should be a good sized spark to indicate output. If there isn't, then something is wrong with either your inspection or assembly. Check the brushes to see that they are seated properly. If the generator is generating, the voltage regulator or wiring is at fault. You will find the voltage regulator somewhere under the hood. It is the sealed box with a number of wires attached to it. Although we call it the voltage regulator, this little box also looks after current regulation and acts as a switch so that the battery can not discharge through the generator when the car is idling or not running.

See if the cover will come off. Do a visual inspection of the units inside. The unit that has the heavy wire connected to it is the cutout relay. These points should be open when the car is not running. The other two units should have the points closed. If the points are dirty or burnt, they can be cleaned with fine wet and dry sandpaper. If they are badly corroded, the regulator should be removed and replaced.

The cost of repairing your own regulator is not warranted because adjustments have to be made with proper equipment and you won't be any dollars ahead. Replace with a rebuilt or new stock when in doubt.

If you decide to clean the points, run a lint-free cloth dampened with alcohol between them so that all foreign material is removed. Don't touch the adjustment of the springs or any of those little screws that look so inviting. There is little that can go wrong with the regulator except for the points. Make sure that the generator is working before you cause yourself some expensive problems.

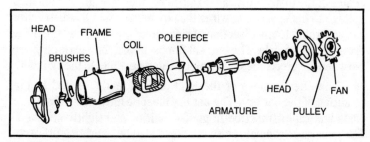

Fig. 13-4. Generator identification.

On cars that use an alternator, you will find no means of lubricating the bearings. They are prelubricated and when they get to the noise stage it is time for replacement. With cars that use alternators, disconnect the battery ground strap before you attempt any service. Endplate bearings are not difficult to replace, but the drive end-bearings might have to have the pulley pulled before you can get at it.

If you don't have the proper pullers, have the work done at a shop. Brushes are much easier to replace and on some makes it might not be necessary to remove the alternator from the car. Diodes are the cause of many charging problems and they should be tested when the alternator is suspect. Have the balance of the parts checked at an electrical shop at the same time.

Depending on the cost of repair and the cost of a rebuilt, decide on the route you want to go (Fig. 13-5). Properly tension the belt and start the engine. If there is a no charge situation indicated, check the regulator. Some makes (Chrysler) use a fusible wire that might have melted through. Other makes might need regulator service and this should be done at an electrical shop.

Ignition System Service

The purpose of the ignition system is to ignite the compressed fuel air mixture in the combustion chamber. When the ignition switch is turned on and the engine started, the breaker points in the distributor are closed by the action of the distributor cam.

Battery current flows through the primary windings of the igniton coil and creates a magnetic field. The rotation of the cam causes the points to open and the current in the primary windings stops flowing, the magnetic field collapses and a high voltage is induced in the secondary windings in the coil. This high voltage passes from the ignition coil through the high tension lead to the center of the distributor cap. From here, the rotor directs the high voltage to the spark plug wires that are arranged in the distributor cap according to the direction of rotation of the rotor and the firing order of the engine. The current jumps across the spark-plug gap between the electrodes of the plug to ignite the fuel in the cylinder.

The effectiveness of the ignition is directly related to the condition of the battery. The battery must be fully charged and the posts and cables must be in good condition and tightly attached. The generator-regulator circuit should also be operating properly to produce the necessary system voltage during operation.

Let's do the primary winding checks first. If there are signs of cracking, burning or corrosion, replace and clean. The terminals must be clean and tight. The coil must be connected into the primary circuit so that the coil polarity (+ or −) marks correspond to those of the battery. Some coils are marked "Batt" and "Dist" so check the wiring to see that it is in the right place.

To check the coil polarity, use the lead pencil test. Bare about one-half inch of a soft lead pencil. Pull one spark plug lead and hold it about one-fourth of an inch from a good ground. Start the engine and run it at a fast idle. Hold the pencil lead in the center of the spark. If the spark flares out on the ground side of the pencil lead, polarity is okay. If the flare is on the spark plug wire side, polarity is reversed and the coil wires should be changed about.

When replacing the coil, use those that match the rating and polarity of the system. Reversed polarity or an improperly rated coil will result in poor voltage output and can cause hard starting, missing and poor overall performance.

To check the breaker points, remove the distributor cap. With the ignition switch off, separate the breaker points and check the condition. A dull gray color is normal. Burned, badly eroded and pitted points should be replaced. Check the movable breaker arm rubbing block and pivot point for wear. Check the cam surface for a worn condition. If points are not worn excessively, they can be cleaned with a fine-cut point file. Do not alter the shape of the points. Run a piece of smooth paper between the points to remove any metal particles. It is difficult to set old points with a feeler gauge; a dwell meter should be used.

If you are going to replace the points, it is more convenient to remove the distributor from the engine. Mark the position of the

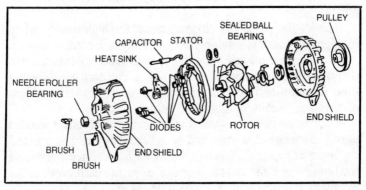

Fig. 13-5. Alternator identification.

rotor and distributor housing before removal. To prevent cranking the engine while the distributor is out, remove the battery ground cable. If you want to replace the points on the engine, fine, but plug any hole around the breaker plate so that you don't drop any screws in or you will end up taking the distributor out.

Check the main shaft for wear in the top bushing. If it is excessive, either the shaft or the bushing(s) must be replaced. See that you can get parts before you take the distributor apart. Other areas to check are the gear for chipping or wear and the centrifugal advance unit.

Remove the used points and clean the mounting area. If there is metal transfer on the points, have the condenser checked for capacity; resistance and leakage. Install the new points and condenser if required and check the points for alignment. If the points are flat, they should come together so that the entire surface touches at once.

If they are both convex or if one is convex and the other flat, contact should be in the center. Bend the stationary point bracket *not* the movable arm. To set the point gap, use a clean flat feeler gauge. Turn the distributor cam until the breaker arm rubbing block is on the highest tip of one of the lobes. Loosen the locking screw just enough so that you can move the points. Set to manufacturer's instructions and tighten locking screw. Check primary wire, condenser wire and breaker plate ground wire to make certain that all are correctly and firmly attached. Wires must be free of moving parts (Fig. 13-6).

Lubricate the cam with high temperature grease or with the cam lubricant supplied with some new point sets. Moisten the felt wick oiler and the breaker arm pivot pin with 20W oil. If an outside reservoir is used, oil or grease sparingly. Do *not* get any oil on the points.

Check the secondary circuit. Inspect the high tension wires for signs of cracking, swelling, burning and other deterioration. If your system is using resistance wire, an ohmmeter can be used to determine if the resistance is within limits. Pull each wire, one at a time, from the distributor cap and inspect the cap towers for signs of corrosion, burning or flashover.

Corrosion can be removed with sandpaper around a wooden pencil. Burning or flashover will be indicated by a carbon path and cap must be replaced. When replacing each wire, make sure that the terminal is clean and the wire is shoved into each tower to the full depth. Use new boots when replacing a cap.

Inspect the inside of the distributor cap for signs of flashover, cracking, eroded terminals or a worn and damaged rotor button. If terminal posts require cleaning, use sandpaper. For any other cause replace the cap. Check the rotor for a tight fit on the distributor shaft. Inspect for burning on the tip and contact spring. It is probably good sense to replace the rotor when you replace the cap. Some rotors pull up while others are held in place by screws. When installing, make certain the rotor is aligned with the flat on the distributor shaft and that it is pressed down fully. A rotor improperly installed can be broken and the distributor cap damaged.

If the distributor was removed, align with the marks and press the body into place. If the rotor turns out of the marked position, pull the distributor up far enough to disengage the gear. Move the rotor far enough to compensate for turning and press down again. Start the engine. If you have a dwell meter, adjust the points as required before setting the timing. Use a timing light and set to specifications.

You should do spark plug service when you service the distributor. Spark plug failure can be caused by a burnt insulator or electrode, incorrect heat range, engine overheating, lean fuel mixture, leakage between the electrode and the insulator or

Fig. 13-6. Use a flat feeler gauge to set a point gap.

improper installation of the plug. Other causes included fouled or shorted plugs, incorrect heat range, excessive engine oil consumption, defective ignition wiring, or loss of compression due to valve failure.

Spark plugs should be cleaned and gapped at 5000 mile intervals if you have the equipment to do the job. You can get along with a small air-operated abrasive cleaner, but if you have to get this service done at a shop you should consider replacing the plugs instead (Fig. 13-7).

Remove the spark plug wires from the spark plugs. Note the location. Blow out any foreign material around the base of the plugs. Use a spark plug socket with the rubber insert to loosen all the plugs about one turn.

Start the engine and blow out any remaining particles. Remove the plugs and the gaskets and keep the plugs in order so that the plug condition can be related to the cylinder that it came from. Normal spark plug appearance will be a gray or tan on the insulator deposit. A dry black fuel deposit known as fuel fouling can be caused by wrong spark heat range, high fuel level in the carburetor, clogged air cleaner, stuck heat riser valve, etc.

If the plug is covered with wet, black deposits, this is an oil fouling condition caused by an excessive amount of oil reaching the cylinders. Worn rings, valve guides and valve seals are common causes.

After studying the plugs for unusual conditions, wash them in clean solvent and blow dry. Do *not* use a wire wheel. Use an abrasive to clean away all deposits and rock the plug to expose all areas to the abrasive. Blow the plug clean of all abrasive. Use a hand wire brush to remove all carbon from the plug threads. File the end of the inner electrode flat, the inside of the side electrode flat and the end square. Set the gap by bending the side electrode and check with a wire gauge. Unless the plug is new, the flat gauge will not give accurate results because of electrode wear.

If you found during examination that the old plugs were fouled out, indicating a cold heat range or they were overheated indicating too hot a plug, check a spark plug to see if you have the proper plugs in the engine. The heat range of a plug is very important to proper engine operation. This term refers to the plug's ability to transfer the heat at the firing tip to the cooling system of the engine. This is determined by the distance the heat must travel and it is controlled by the length of the insulator from the tip to the sealing ring. Usually, the longer the insulator the hotter the plug.

150

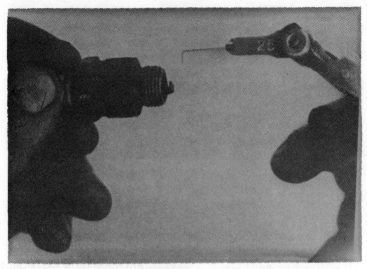

Fig. 13-7. Checking a new spark plug gap.

Generally, an engine which operates at fast speeds or heavy loads will require a cold plug so that the heat will transfer faster. A hot plug will be used in an engine that operates at low or idle speeds most of the time. Hot plugs will burn off the deposits that occur in this type of operation. For normal engine operations, a plug that is somewhere between hot and cold is used.

Replace the plugs and tighten until snug. Use a torque wrench to final tighten. In the absence of a torque wrench, give the plug one-half to three-fourths of a turn beyond snug. Wipe the insulators and attach the plug wires in the correct order.

If you are still having problems with engine operation, go over the trouble shooting and zero in on the component causing the problem. If you have a service center in the area that provides an oscilloscope readout, you can get accurate information on all parts of the ignition system and then do the service yourself. Remember, it is not good sense to do a tune-up if the engine isn't sound.

Chapter 14
Fuel System Troubleshooting

It's a beautiful day, the gas gauge reads full and you are just burning up the highway. You pass the last checkpoint and you are far ahead of anyone else. Then without prior warning the engine and the vehicle coast to a stop. The engine turns over with the cranking motor but it will not start. What happened? You try the spark plug wire test and there is enough spark to light up any fuel mixture. The engine just won't start. Don't run the battery down. Do some quick fuel system troubleshooting.

First and foremost, disregard the reading on the fuel gauge. Check the fuel tank because it is seldom that the starting problems are caused by the carburetor itself. Many of the problems which are traced to the fuel system are the result of an empty fuel tank. See if the tank is dry and whether it is leaking or not. No matter what your uncle says, buttonhead, don't use a match to find out.

If the tank is dry on the outside, it is probably not leaking. If it is dry on the inside, you know the problem and the solution. If the tank has fuel in it, try to trace the problem. Check the fuel tank cap for a vent hole and see that it is open. If the gas tank has a drain plug on the bottom of it, unscrew it and make sure that you have fuel at this point and not water.

Older cars have the tendancy to shed rust flakes in the gas tank. If this problem occurs regularly, then you know what to do. You might consider sealing the inside of the tank with one of the products on the market. If the tank is in very poor condition, the best solution is replacement with a new tank. Flaking will eventually lead to carburetor problems. Fix it once and fix it right.

Similar flaking can occur at the vaccum tank. If you are having this problem, fix it. The use of an inline gasoline fuel filter might work if it is difficult to get a new gasoline tank. There are a number of fuel feed systems, but the three most popular are the gravity, the vacuum and gravity, and the engine-operated fuel pump. Remember, these systems must have a source of supply and that is the gasoline tank. Make sure you have fuel in it.

Gravity Systems

The simplest method of bringing fuel to the carburetor is the gravity system. It consists of placing the supply above the level of the carburetor and letting the fuel down by gravity (Fig. 14-1).

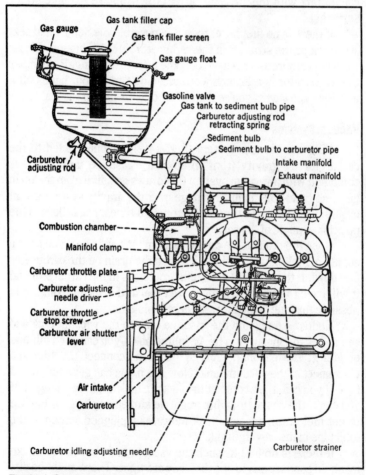

Fig. 14-1. Gravity fuel system.

Turn the fuel tap to the *on* position and if there is a fuel bowl drain open it also. Position a container to catch the fuel and beware of the hot exhaust system. Don't smoke while making these tests.

Fuel must drain out. If it doesn't, the fuel line, fuel tap or the sediment bowl is plugged and it will have to be cleaned. If the fuel flow is okay, remove the fuel line at the carburetor. With the fuel bowl drain closed, see if there is a full pipe of fuel. If there isn't, remove this line and examine it for blockage or kinks.

If the fuel flow is okay, connect the fuel line and open the fuel bowl drain plug in the carburetor. If the fuel drains out, it is possible that one of the jets in the carburetor is plugged and fuel cannot mix with the air. The carburetor will have to come off for servicing.

If there is no fuel here, then it is possible the needle and seat are stuck or the strainer in the carburetor inlet is plugged. Either way, the carburetor will have to come off for servicing. Remember that carburetor is a French word meaning "keep your hands off if you don't know what you're doing." Obtain the proper manual.

Vacuum Systems

With the vacuum system (Fig. 14-2), gasoline is fed to the carburetor by gravity from an auxiliary gasoline tank which is combined with a vacuum system that draws gasoline from the main gasoline tank. The main advantage over the gravity system is that gasoline will be fed to the carburetor at all times, regardless of the position or angle of the car.

Open the drain valve on the vacuum tank and see if you have a supply of fuel this far. If there is, open the drain on the carburetor fuel bowl. If there is fuel here, the problem is in the carburetor and it will have to serviced. If there isn't fuel at the vacuum tank, it is possible that one of the fuel strainers is plugged.

Undo the line from the gasoline tank to the vacuum tank and see if—by forcing air into the gasoline tank—you can get a full line of fuel at the gasoline tank. If you can, connect the line and disconnect at the vacuum tank. Now see if you can get a full line of fuel. If you can, the screen at the vacuum tank might be plugged. If you can't, the connecting line might be kinked or plugged. Failure to get fuel at the gasoline tank indicates a plugged screen at the inlet pipe in the gasoline tank.

If there is no fuel through the vacuum tank, check the intake manifold connections to see that they are tight. There might be dirt under the flapper valve that prevents it from seating airtight.

Remove the plug at the top of the tank and pour some gasoline into the tank. This will clean the flapper valve and cause it to seat better. If the engine will run when you prime the tank this way, the problem is in the vacuum tank and it will have to be serviced. Make sure the fuel is getting to the tank.

Force Feed Systems

The force feed system (Fig. 14-3) uses an engine operated fuel pump which pumps fuel through tubing from the gasoline tank to the carburetor. The fuel pump is operated by a special cam on the camshaft. Generally, the problem with this method of fuel delivery is caused by a plugged filter, a defective fuel pump or a break in the line from the fuel pump to the fuel tank.

Start at the tank and disconnect the fuel line. You will have to get under the car. While you are under the car, check the entire fuel line for kinks or breaks that could prevent the fuel from reaching the fuel pump.

If you are not too keen on getting under the car, you can try a different technique. But you must be prepared for it. Make up some sort of rubber extension tube that you can slip on the fuel line which attaches to the fuel pump. If you draw on the tube, you can make a fairly good analysis in addition to getting a taste of gasoline. All at the same price. This doesn't sound too appetizing and it can be dangerous. If you can't get towed and if you can't tell the mechanic what's wrong, then you are going to stay just about where you are.

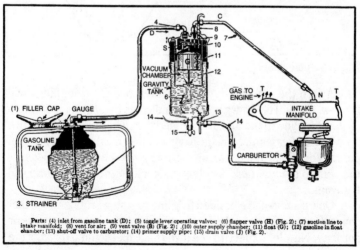

Parts: (4) inlet from gasoline tank (D); (5) toggle lever operating valves; (6) flapper valve (H) (Fig. 2); (7) suction line to intake manifold; (8) vent for air; (9) vent valve (B) (Fig. 2); (10) outer supply chamber; (11) float (G); (12) gasoline in float chamber; (13) shut-off valve to carburetor; (14) primer supply pipe; (15) drain valve (J) (Fig. 2).

Fig. 14-2. Vacuum fuel system.

155

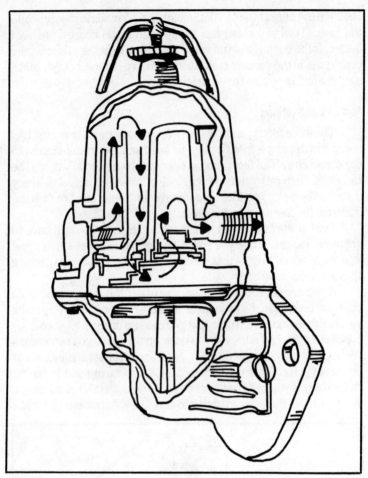

Fig. 14-3. Fuel pump.

Attach the tube and if you draw on it one of three things will happen. Air will be drawn up which indicates that the tank is empty or the steel line to the tank is corroded through. Fuel will be drawn up which indicates the line is okay and the problem is at the fuel pump. Very little fuel drawn up indicates that the line is plugged or the vent to the fuel tank is not open. Remove the gas tank cap and try again.

On cars that use a braided flex line or a short rubber hose that connects the fuel line to the fuel pump, check the hose for cracks or porosity. Now let's check to see if you have fuel coming through the pump.

Disconnect the fuel line at the carburetor. This is the line that comes from the fuel pump. Use a container to catch the gasoline. Be wary of the possibility of fire. Crank the engine with the ignition off. If this is not possible, ground either the distributor side of the coil using a short "jumper" wire or remove the center high tension lead out of the distributor cap and ground it. Ground means to connect the wire to the block so that it cannot spark. This is very important because raw fuel will be flowing in the engine compartment and the chance of fire is high. Remember that fire travels faster then the fire truck.

A full line of fuel should pulse out of the line if the fuel pump is okay. If no fuel flows and there was fuel to the pump, then the pump is defective. On some cars, a *vapor lock* will stop the flow of fuel. If you can douse the pump with cold water or cool it with wet cloths, you might be able to get the fuel moving.

If you find the fuel dripping out of the fuel pump body casing vent holes, it is evident that the pump has to be replaced. If adequate fuel flows to the carburetor and the engine does not start, you will have to check whether fuel is getting through the carburetor.

Remove the air cleaner. If the outside of the carburetor is not wet with fuel, then probably the inside is working okay. If the caruretor is of the type that has an accelerator pump, you should be able to operate the linkage by hand. See if there is a good stream of fuel through the discharge holes and into the carburetor throat.

If there is no fuel at the discharge holes, it is possible that fuel is not getting into the carburetor. This could be due to a stuck needle and seat or a plugged internal fuel filter. The carburetor internal passage ways could be plugged. Try to prime the carburetor and see if the engine will start. For this, you will need some fuel in a separate container. Open the throttle linkage and pour a bit down the carburetor. Turn the ignition on and start the engine. If it runs and then quits, you have carburetor problems. Do not prime the engine while turning it over with the cranking motor.

If you have an internal filter, remove it and examine it. If it is plugged, replace the fuel line and start the engine. If the engine continues to run, the filter was the problem. If the engine doesn't run, it is possible that the needle and seat are inoperative. To examine the needle and seat assembly, you will have to remove the top of the carburetor. If you decide to do this on the car, plug the carburetor throat with a cloth so that a screw will not drop into the engine. If the carburetor is easy to remove, you might decide to take it off the engine. With the top removed, there must be fuel in the fuel bowl. If there isn't, check the fuel inlet for blockage and the needle and seat assembly for being stuck in the closed position. If there is fuel in the bowl, then the carburetor passage ways are plugged and they will have to be serviced (Fig. 14-4).

If you find that the outside of the carburetor is wet with gasoline and the engine will not run, you have a situation where there is too much gasoline. This is due to internal carburetor problems with the float and needle and seat assembly. You will have to remove the top of the carburetor and see why the needle and seat assembly are not shutting off the fuel supply. This could be due to dirt, worn needle and seat or the float is leaking and has gasoline in it.

Check to see if the choke plate is in the full open position. If it isn't, before you remove the top of the carburetor move it to open and try to start the engine. Don't give it any more gas and see that the throttle plate is also full open. In other words, gas pedal to the floor. If the engine will run, there is no need to work on the carburetor.

The carburetor will have to be serviced when there is an indicated fuel problem at any of the speeds or when accelerating and additional fuel is not supplied. Remember, service the carburetor only after you have made certain that fuel is getting that far.

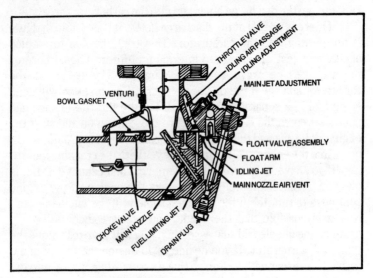

Fig. 14-4. Carburetor identification.

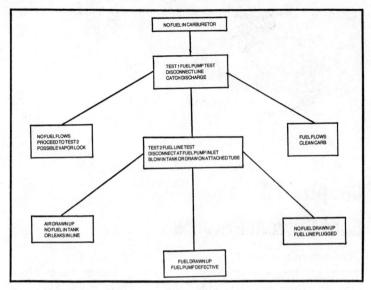

Fig. 14-5. Fuel system tests.

Cars that have not run for some length of time should first have all the stale fuel drained out of the gasoline tank. Then the fuel line should be disconnected at the gasoline tank and at the fuel pump inlet side. Force air pressure into the tank to blow out any sludge and varnish. You don't want to force this mess up to the fuel pump. Force air into the fuel line from the fuel pump side to the gasoline tank and blow this line clean.

If the pump is operative, you should be able to get fuel to the carburetor. To save the battery you might force air pressure into the tank and get fuel running at the fuel pump outlet. Priming the engine will probably get it started, but keeping it going is another matter. Carburetors that have varnish in them are not going to operate properly. If you were lucky enough to get the fuel pump running, why push your luck. Service the carburetor.

Remember, an engine that has not run for some time should have the oil and the coolant changed. Make sure that the pump hasn't seized and that the coolant doesn't leak into the oil. Check the oil levels in the transmission and differential. Lubricate any points on the drive and steering train. Check tire pressure. If you still want to get the car going well, it's up to you.

It might be better to completely go over the car and know that it's good rather than start and remove all doubt. In other words trailer it home. See Fig. 14-5.

Chapter 15
Fuel System Service

The units of the fuel system include the gas tank, fuel line, fuel pump, gas gauge, carburetor, air cleaner, intake mainfold and exhaust system. Some systems include a vacuum tank also.

Fuel Supply

The gas tank is usually located at the rear of the chassis and can hold from 10 to 20 gallons of gasoline. It must be vented to the atmosphere in order to maintain pressure on the fuel in the tank. A gauge of some type is used to inform the driver of the amount of fuel in the tank.

A gas tank that has excessive amounts of water, dirt and rust flaking must be removed for cleaning. First, you must drain out the fuel. A fuel drain is provided on some tanks and in other cases you will have to siphon the fuel out. Place the gasoline in closed metal containers and be careful of fire. You might remove the battery ground strap to prevent the possibility of shorting the gas gauge wire on some models.

Disconnect the fuel lines and remove the gas tank. Gas tanks that fit in the cowl and form part of the dash will have to be removed carefully so that the paint isn't marked. On this style, a special wrench is used to remove the gas gauge. Drain out any remaining gas and inspect the interior of the tank. If the tank is rusted it should be replaced. If not, clean it thoroughly by steaming. Tanks that are rusty, but not rusted through, can be cured of rust flaking by coating the inside of the tank with a plastic tank sealer.

A leaking gas tank can be repaired by soldering or brazing, but it must be thoroughly steamed out first. Check the cost of repair. It might be cheaper to get a new tank. You might decide to try some of the types of chemical welding that are available on the market and repair the tank while it is on the car. Test the repair before putting the tank back. Tanks that have dents in the bottoms can be repaired by filling the tank completely full of water and plugging all the openings except where the fuel line connects. Apply air pressure through this opening and the tank should straighten out.

To clean the fuel line, disconnect it at the fuel pump end and the gas tank. Direct a blast of air from the fuel pump end toward the gas tank. Blow until clean. If the lines remain restricted, check for dents or kinks. Remove the damaged section and replace with a new section of tubing or hose. Use air to clean the fuel line that connects the fuel pump to the carburetor. A short flexible hose is usually placed at the fuel pump end of the line from the tank. This hose absorbs the vibration in the line between the engine and the car frame. The hose can become porous or crack so make an inspection at this point before you can condemn the fuel pump.

Fuel filters are placed in the fuel line between the fuel pump and the carburetor to remove dirt and water from the fuel. See that they are not plugged before you test the fuel pump. Tighten the pump diaphragm cover and the mounting bolts. Inspect the lines for kinks, dents or leaks. See that there *is* gas in the tank. Clean or replace the fuel filters. Check the gas tank vent and cap. Tighten the filter bowl cover.

The fuel pump should be checked for leaks, output pressure, flow volume and inlet volume. To do this, you must have a combination pressure and vacuum gauge or you could use a regular manifold vacuum gauge and any low-reading pressure gauge.

Remove the inlet line at the carburetor and attach the pressure gauge. Hold the tester at carburetor level. If the engine will run, let it do so using the remaining fuel in the carburetor. The pressure should read 3 to 4 pounds, but check the manufacturer's specifications depending on what make of pump you are testing.

To do the flow volume test, you need a container to catch the fuel. *Don't* let it spray under the hood because the chances of fire are excellent. You should get about a quart of fuel in one minute at 500 rpm. If you ran the carburetor dry in the pressure test, then it is evident you won't be able to idle the engine unless you get fuel to the carburetor.

When the pressure and the volume do not meet specifications, check the pump inlet vacuum. Disconnect the fuel line from the pump inlet flex line. Attach the vacuum gauge to the flex line. Cap the gas line if it leaks. Disconnect the presure line at the carburetor and place it in a container.

Start the engine and let it idle until the gauge reads the highest reading. About ten inches of vacuum is normal. Stop the engine, the reading should hold steady. This indicates that the pump valves, diaphragm, flex line and bowl gasket are airtight. If the reading is below 10 inches or if it drops off rapidly when the engine is stopped, remove the flex line and attach the gauge directly to the pump. Test it again and if there is a low reading or fall off continues, the pump is defective. If the reading holds, the flex line should be replaced.

When the vacuum test indicates that the pump and the flex line are not leaking, test the entire inlet system. Remove the line at the gas tank and attach the gauge. Start the engine. If the vacuum drops or falls rapidly, an air leak in the inlet system is indicated.

If the fuel pump on your vehicle is of the combination fuel/vacuum booster type, you should also check the vacuum booster side. A defective booster pump can cause extremely heavy oil consumption. A cracked diaphragm or a faulty valve will allow the engine vacuum to draw oil and oil vapor from the crankcase directly into the intake manifold.

To test, disconnect the line from the vacuum pump to the intake manifold. Remove the line from the windshield wiper or other accessories and connect the vacuum gauge at this point. Run the engine at about 1000 rpm and not the vacuum reading. The reading should be 8 inches or more. When the engine is stopped, the reading should hold steady or fall off slowly.

You can buy rebuilt pumps as an exchange service or you can get a fuel pump repair kit for your pump and repair it yourself. The pumps on newer cars are of the sealed type and need special equipment for rebuilding them. Leave these alone. If you can not get a kit, it is possible to make a new diaphragm out of a neoprene coated nylon material which does a good job.

The valves can be washed if they are stuck, but you cannot rebuild them. Put the pump back together and try it on the bench before you put it back on the motor. You can do the same tests by working the rocker arm back and forth with your hand. Other service consists of rocker arm build-up and replacing the pull rod oil seal.

Make sure that you bolt the pump cover onto the pump body in its proper location. Marking before disassembly is the best idea. The rocker arm pin must be a snug fit in the body to prevent oil leaks. Various filters are used with fuel pumps. If they cannot be cleaned they should be replaced. Clean or change them and when fuel pump problems occur check the filters to see that they are clean. Some carburetors incorporate a filter in the fuel inlet and these should be cleaned or replaced before you have dirt in the carburetor itself.

The condition called *vapor lock* is caused by the fuel in the pump or lines being heated and starting to vaporize. This causes tiny air bubbles and when enough bubbles are formed the fuel flow is reduced or even stopped. Running fuel lines too close to the exhaust manifold, excessive looping and bending of the fuel line, or leaving off a heat shield can all cause vapor lock. Determine the reason and make the necessary repairs.

Vacuum Tank

The air vent on the tank allows atmospheric pressure to be maintained on the fuel in the lower chamber so that there will be a constant supply to the carburetor. The vent also serves to prevent an overflow of gasoline when descending steep grades. If the vent tube (Fig. 15-1) overflows regularly, check for the following conditions.

The vent in the main gasoline filler cap might be stopped up or it might be too small. Enlarge or clean it out to one-eighth of an inch diameter. The bottom of the tank must be not less than 3 inches above the carburetor. Raise the tank if necessary.

If gasoline leaks from other than the vent tube, check the following.

There might be a leak in the outer wall of the tank and it will have to be repaired. If the tank is rusted through and you cannot get another tank, try some gas tank sealer.

The carburetor fitting in the bottom of the tank might be loose or the drain valve is loose and leaks. Repair or replace as necessary.

There might be a leak in the fuel line leading from the gas tank. If you find that fuel is not feeding to the carburetor, remove the inner tank and see if it is dry. If it is dry, check the gasoline strainer or the fuel line first. See that the float has not developed a leak and that it is too heavy to rise and close the vacuum valve. This will allow gasoline to be drawn into the manifold and cause a choking condition. The flapper valve must be free and clean so that it will seal on its seat. Check the manifold connections to see they are tight and not drawing air.

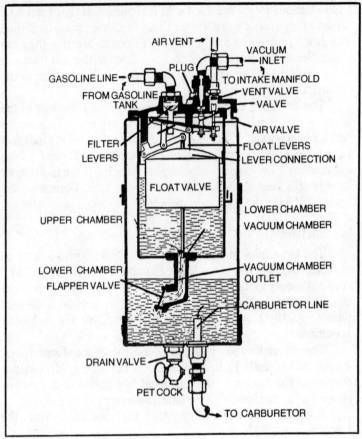

Fig. 15-1. Vacuum tank identification.

To repair a leaky float, use a small amount of solder and test it by dipping in hot water. If no bubbles are seen, the float is air tight. See that the gear mechanism is free and not binding. See that you have clean fuel coming from the gas tank and that all the strainers and screens are clean.

Carburetors

Check the compression, ignition and fuel system before you start working on the carburetor unless you know for a fact that the trouble is in the carburetor. There are a number of adjustments that can be made with the carburetor on the engine while others will have to be made on disassembly (Fig. 15-2).

The carburetor vaporizes and mixes the gasoline and the air in the proper proportions necessary for starting, idling, acceleration and power at the various speeds. By volume, it takes about 10,000 gallons of air for each gallon of gasoline or by weight one part of gasoline to 15 parts of air.

This fuel/air ratio is controlled by jets, air bleeds and valves. A jet can be integral with the casting or a separate part fitted into a passage way in the casting. The jet has a calibrated hole through which the fuel flows. Each circuit in the carburetor has one or more jets to control the flow of fuel.

The air bleeds are small openings that conduct air from the air horn to the various circuits. By mixing air with fuel, the fuel is partially atomized before it reaches the discharge point. Valves of various types control the flow of fuel and air. Needle type valves control the flow of fuel and butterfly type valves control the flow of air.

There is a restriction in the carburetor called the *venturi*. Its purpose is to create a partial vacuum in the air passage. When the same amount of air moves through the venturi, as through the rest of the passage, the velocity of the air will be the greatest at the narrowest point. A discharge nozzle is mounted here and the faster the air moves through the venturi the greater the amount of fuel will be drawn out of the nozzle into the air stream. Some

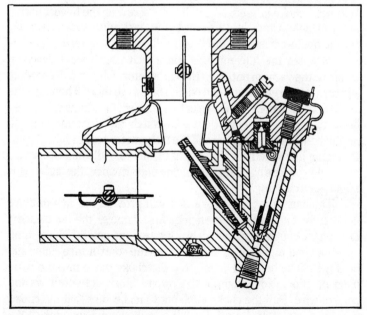

Fig. 15-2. Carburetor disassembled.

carburetors use dual or triple venturies to produce the low pressure area in a desired place in the air passage way.

Carburetor Circuits

Before you do any work on the carburetor circuits, see that you have a specification chart at hand for the particular carburetor you will be adjusting. If you are planning further work and adjustments, see that you have a repair kit for the particular work you want to do. Have a clean work area and the necessary tools and gauges to do the job.

Follow the manual step-by-step and you will do a responsible overhaul. If you take some short cuts you are going to do the job many times over. Analyze the carburetor problem and troubleshoot the cause before you start the repair.

Do the idle speed adjustment first and then you can set the idle mixture. Bring the engine to normal operating temperature. If the automatic transmission is used, see if it should be in neutral or drive. If drive is used, set the handbrake and also block the wheels. Remove the aircleaner and see that the choke is fully open. Attach a tachometer. Locate the idle speed adjusting screw. It will probably be on or near the throttle shaft. Turn the screw in to increase the rpm and out to decrease the rpm. Adjust to proper speed. If an automatic choke is used, adjust the idle screw on the lowest part of the fast idle cam. In this way, the fast idle speed will be automatically adjusted as the choke pulls the cam upward.

Now set the idle mixture and attach your reliable vacuum gauge to the vacuum outlet on the carburetor. Observe the reading and turn the screw in until the engine begins to miss. Then turn the needle out until the engine starts to roll. Turn the screw in half way between these two conditions and watch the vacuum gauge to produce the highest reading and the tachometer to the highest rpm. Reset the idle speed if it changes. If turning the idle mixture screw in or out produces no change in engine performance, the carburetor might need cleaning.

To adjust a manual choke that will provide the rich mixture needed for starting a cold engine, first remove the air cleaner. Loosen the choke lever swivel block screw and pull the choke knob out about one-eighth of an inch. Tighten the control wire clamp and hold the choke lever so as to force the choke valve into the wide open position. Now, tighten the swivel block set screw on the control wire. Pull the choke knob out to make sure that the choke valve is completely closed. Push the choke knob in and the choke valve should be open. A fast idling device is used to provide for faster idling speed during warm-up and to prevent stalling. It might need adjustment, but make sure that you have the proper procedure for this one.

To adjust an automatic choke, follow the carburetor manual instructions. If you find that the carburetor is dirty and sticky, clean it in carbon solvent or you will have a choke problem. In an automatic choke, the various stages of choke valve opening are controlled by the combination of a temperature-operated thermostatic spring, the engine vacuum and the air flow through the throat of the carburetor.

When the throttle is suddenly opened, it causes the engine vacuum to suddenly drop. You have probably noticed this on the action of vacuum type windshield wipers that do not have a booster; they come to a stop. In the carburetor, the result is a lean mixture reaching the cylinders and causing a drop in engine power. To prevent this, an accelerator operated pump discharges a stream of gasoline into the air stream.

To check this pump action, remove the air cleaner and open the throttle quickly from idle to full open (with the engine stopped). Depending on pump design, one or more streams of gas should discharge through the pump discharge nozzle in the air horn. If little or no gas output is noticed, the accelerator pump piston leather could be cracked or worn. The check valves or the discharge feed system could be plugged. The carburetor should be removed for cleaning.

The most important circuit in the carburetor is the float circuit because it controls the height of the gasoline level in the bowl and nozzle. A high fuel level will result in poor gas mileage, spark plug fouling, crankcase dilution and all-around poor performance. A low level will cause splitting, bucking and loss of power.

The float bowl acts as a reservoir to hold a supply of gasoline throughout the entire range of engine performance. The float level is checked by either measuring from some portion of the float to the cover (use of an inspection plug) or by using a gauge designed for the purpose. When the needle valve is off its seat, gasoline flows into the float bowl. The float is connected to a lever and a pivot. As the float rises, the lever bears against the lower end of the needle valve and causes it to be lifted upward into the needle valve seat. This closes off the flow of gasoline into the float bowl (Fig. 15-3).

To service the float or the needle and seat, you should remove the carburetor from the engine. If you decide to service this circuit

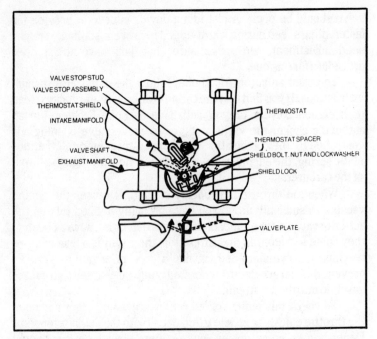

Fig. 15-3. Manifold heat control valve identification.

with the carburetor on—and if the carburetor is mounted above the intake manifold (down-draft) as opposed to the carburetor mounted below the intake manifold (up-draft)—plug the main body with a cloth so that you don't drop any bolts into the engine. Think of the damage a loose piece could do in the engine and you'll see that the little time you might save is hardly worth it.

The carburetor usually consists of three separate castings: the upper, called the air horn; the center, called the main body and fuel bowl; and the lower, called the throttle body. When two castings are used, the air horn and main body are in one casting. The passageway in the carburetor through which the air passes is called the throat. The air horn, to which the air cleaner is attached and where the air enters the carburetor, includes the choke assembly. The main body includes the venturi and most of the carburetor circuits. The throttle body includes the throttle valve, idle mixture and idle speed adjustment, and the parts that attach the carburetor to the manifold.

If you find the carburetor flooding—meaning that the gasoline is not being shut-off inside the carburetor—then you can readily suspect the float or the needle and seat assembly.

On some carburetors, when you remove the air horn the float will be attached to it. On others, the float will remain in the main body and fuel bowl. Remove the float and shake it to see if it has any fuel in it. This would indicate that it is leaking. The float must be airtight. To check it, submerge it in water that you have heated to just below the boiling point. If bubbles show then leaks are indicated.

Solder it with a minimum of solder so that it doesn't get too heavy. Remove the seat and check it against the needle. Replace them if they are worn or grooved. Check the float for easy movement and set the float level as per the manufacturer's specifications. Put the air horn back and check to see if the flooding condition continues. If it does, you haven't done your work too well and you might as well remove the carburetor for cleaning and inspection.

It is possible that you might have a fuel pump that is putting out too much pressure and thereby causing a flooding situation. Pumps usually don't get stronger as they get older.

Before you take the carburetor apart, see that you have screwdrivers that will fit the slots properly and use the right size. Some carburetors will need special wrenches which will prevent damage to the parts. See that you have the specifications for settings and adjustments.

Disassemble the carburetor. If you have carburetor cleaner, soak the parts for the necessary time. Do not soak any of the parts that are made of rubber, leather or fabric. Remove, rinse and blow dry. Blow out all the passageways. Do not probe with a wire, drill or similar tool because you will enlarge the openings. If you can't get a blast of air through, then soak again.

Inspect all parts for cracks. Examine the throttle and choke shafts for wear and out-of-roundness. Check for stripped fasteners and the castings where they fit in. Check the idle mixture screws for grooves. Check the needle and seat for same. Check the float. Secure a minor or major overhaul kit. On assembly, do not use gasket cement unless it is specified. Tighten all pieces properly and make the right adjustments. Clean the mounting area on the manifold and use a new gasket. Attach the necessary lines, hoses and linkages. Leave the aircleaner off for now and start the engine checking for leaks and adjustments.

Check the manifold heat control valve to see if it is stuck in either the open or closed position. This valve is sometimes called the heat riser valve and it will stick due to excess carbon. When stuck in the open position, slow warmup, carburetor icing and stalling, flat spots during acceleration, or crankcase dilution can occur. If stuck closed, overheating, detonation, burned valves, or warped manifold can result (Fig. 15-4).

See that the shaft is free in its bushings and do not distort the thermostatic spring. Apply some type of carbon dissolvent to the ends of the shaft and slowly work the valve back and forth until free. If the valve is stuck tight, use a small hammer to tap the ends of the shaft until it can be moved by hand. Leave the shaft dry and clean. Do not lubricate with oil.

If you suspect an intake manifold leak, first torque the fasteners. Check for a leak by squirting oil with an oil can along the gasket edge. If a leak exists, the idle speed will change. This is a good place to use the vacuum gauge tester. It will help you set the idle mixture setting and it can also indicate other engine problems.

The air cleaner is mounted on the air horn of the carburetor and does three things. It removes dust particles from the air before they enter the carburetor, it silences the noise of the air rushing into the engine, and it acts as a flame arrester if the engine backfires through the carburetor.

The upper part of the air cleaner contains a ring of filter material such as fine mesh metal threads or ribbons, fiber or special paper. This material provides a fine maze through which the air must pass. Some air cleaners use an oil reservoir over which the incoming air must pass (Fig. 15-5 and 15-6).

Air cleaners should be serviced every time the engine oil is changed. However, if dusty conditions are encountered, the air cleaner element should be cleaned immediately afterward. Remember that the primary purpose of the air cleaner is to keep dust from entering the engine. The element is removed by removing the wing nuts or supporting clamp. The method of cleaning varies with the type of filter material.

If the filter material is made of metal threads or fiber, it can be cleaned in solvent and then blown dry if the oil has not caked or become too gummy. Soak in solvent if necessary. Dip the filter in clean oil and let it drip dry—then reinstall. With air cleaners that use an oil bath, dump the old oil out of the cleaner body, wash it out with solvent and refill with clean oil to the proper mark. Do not overfill. Reinstall the filter element and cleaner body on the engine.

Air cleaners that use a paper element can have the element cleaned by using compressed air and blowing from the center outward. Do not use excessive air pressure because you will rupture the paper and the element will have to be replaced. After cleaning, examine for punctures and if any are noticed discard the element. See that the sealing rings on the upper and lower sides of the element are smooth. They must seal. Clean the top and bottom parts of the filter before assembly. Replace the element if it will not come clean or if you cannot see light through it.

Some air filters are not installed directly on the carburetor, but are connected to the carburetor by a flexible hose. This hose must be connected airtight to both the filter and the carburetor. Also, the hose must not have any rips in it that would admit unfiltered air.

Manifolds And Exhaust System

The intake manifold is a passage that carrys the air-fuel mixture from the carburetor to the engine cylinders. The carburetor mounts on the intake manifold. The intake manifold is mounted on the side of the block on engines that have the valves in the block (L-head) and on the side of the head with engines that have the valves in the head (I-head). On V-2-4-6-8-12-16 engines, the intake manifold is located between the cylinder banks.

The exhaust manifold carries the burned gases away from the engine cylinders. It is made of cast iron and bolted over the exhaust

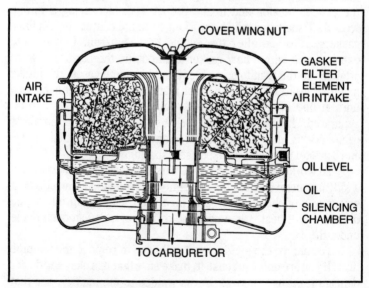

Fig. 15-4. An oil bath type air cleaner.

ports and can provide heat to the intake manifold. This helps to further vaporize the fuel in the intake manifold. On V-type engines, there are two exhaust manifolds—one for each bank of cylinders. The exhaust gases which are both noisy and poisonous must be silenced and moved away from the passenger compartment. The exhaust pipe muffler and tailpipe accomplish this function.

The exhaust pipe is the long pipe that leads from the exhaust manifold to the muffler. The muffler reduces the noise of the exhaust by slowing down the speed of the escaping gases and passing these gases through different passages before allowing them to escape through the tailpipe where they are discharged into the atmosphere. There is very little service for the manifolds except the freeing of the manifold heat control valve. However, there are times that you will have to remove and replace the manifolds such as during engine overhaul, etc.

To remove the mainfolds, first presoak the fasteners and especially the ones that hold the exhaust pipe to the manifold. Remove the carburetor and any braces, tubing, etc. that might be connected. Disconnect the pipe flange, remove the manifold fasteners and take the manifold off. Examine for cracks and see that the sealing surfaces are not warped. If they are, you can use a file to true them up.

When you are installing, all gasket surfaces must be clean and you must use new gaskets. Tighten the attaching bolts or nuts to the proper tension and in the proper sequence using a torque wrench. Usually you will be working from the center out. On thick gaskets, retorque after the engine has been run. Connect the exhaust pipe with a new gasket and hook up the parts that were attached to the manifold. As mentioned in some cases, the intake manifold attaches to the exhaust manifold and is assembled as a unit. If one or the other needs replacing, they will have to be separated. Intake manifolds for V-type engines are similarly removed and installed. Do not drop any bolts into the intake ports and if gasket cement is advised use it sparingly.

To work on the muffler system itself, you should at least have a slitting chisel so that you can relieve the seized connections at either end of the muffler. Use plenty of penetrating oil. If you decide to use heat, remember the danger of using an open flame under the car.

To remove the muffler, you will have to remove the tail pipe first. If you are going to reuse it, make sure that it is okay and do not damage it during removal. If it is welded to the muffler, see that you do not cut it off too short. Use penetrating oil, tap and heat or slit the muffler if the tail pipe is held with a clamp. The same procedure will apply to the front of the muffler. Examine the exhaust pipe and replace if necessary. Always use the proper size pipes and mufflers. The exhaust must get out.

Check the length of the replacement muffler against your old one and if you cannot get the right lengths you will have to use short extensions. Position these properly. Check the muffler for an inlet marking and slide it on the exhaust pipe. Use muffler cement. The joints will slide easier and the there is less danger of leaks. The pipe must enter to the proper depth. Position the muffler clamp so that it will compress the muffler nipple properly—about one-eighth of an inch from the end.

Install the tail pipe and align the tail pipe and muffler. See that there is proper clearance over the rear axle, springs and shocks. Tighten the tail pipe clamp and any of the support brackets. Start the car and check for leaks. If any are found repair them. Exhaust gases contain carbon monoxide. It is a deadly gas and one which you cannot smell or see. Make sure that the joints are leak proof.

Chapter 16
Preventive Maintenance

I have discussed a number of problems and some of the service that can be done. These problems seem to show up with amazing regularity and you are probably familiar with many of them. Now, why is this the case? The reason is that we neglect the simple, routine servicing functions that if performed on a regular basis will allow a vehicle to travel efficiently, safely and reliably. See Table 16-1.

What am I refering to? Preventive maintenance that's what. You can do it with a minimum of tools and time and save maximum money. Let's break this into separate mechanical areas and see what can be done. The areas are: engine, lubrication, fuel, cooling, ignition, battery, wheel alignment, tires, suspension, brakes and driveline.

Get a lubrication and maintenance chart for your vehicle and update it with the new products that are on the market (Fig. 16-1). If you are still using mineral oil, I think you should consider going into the new multi-grade oils. But a word of caution here. New oils can loosen sludge deposits in the engine which will be carried by the oil through the oil passageways. The deposits might block the passageways and result in damage to the engine.

If you have an engine of this type, it might be worth your while to dismantle it and clean it up before you change to a different type of oil. If the oil screen plugs, the engine will have had it. Think this one out. You might remove the oil pan and the valve chamber cover and see if you have a sludge condition.

If you decide to change to the heavy-duty oils and if you know that the oil pan is not sludged up, bring the engine to operating temperature and drain the oil. Change the filter and see that the case is clean. Do not leave any of the other oil in the filter case. Replace with a new filter. Fill the crankcase with the proper weight heavy-duty oil and drive the car about 30 minutes. Keep your eye on the oil pressure gauge and watch for any abnormal fluctuations. Drain this oil out and refill with fresh oil.

If necessary, change the oil filter. You can check by placing a drop of oil on a white blotter and noticing the amount of foreign material. Remember that filters and oil are cheaper than clogging the engine's lubrication system. Heavy-duty oil darkens quickly with very little service. Therefore, color is not a true indicator of the condition of the oil. If the engine has a crankcase ventilation system, see that it is clean and operating properly.

You should change oil at least twice a year, say spring and fall, if you do any driving at all. You're right, oil doesn't wear out, but it does circulate the fine metal abrasives, etc. that will cause engine wear.

Table 16-1. Servicing Checklist.

	CHECK	SERVICE
BRAKE SYSTEM		
Brake fluid	4000 miles	Replace each year
Front wheel bearings		Clean and lubricate
Complete brake system	10,000 miles	Every 16,000 miles
IGNITION & ELECTRICAL		
Minor tune up		5000 inspect and adjust
Major tune up		10,000 replace points, plugs, condenser
COOLING SYSTEM		
Belts, hoses, thermostat	Spring & Fall	Replace parts needed
Pre-winter service	Fall	
CHASSIS SYSTEM		
Suspension, steering exhaust	4000 miles	Replace worn parts
Lubricate Chassis parts	Factory Specifications	
Lubricate Universal joints		
FUEL AND ENGINE SYSTEMS		
All components	Every 6 months	Replace every 12,000 miles
Fuel filter and air filer		Replace every 12,000 miles
PCU valve	4000 miles	Check Factory specs
OIL filter		Check Factory specs
Automatic transmission fluid		

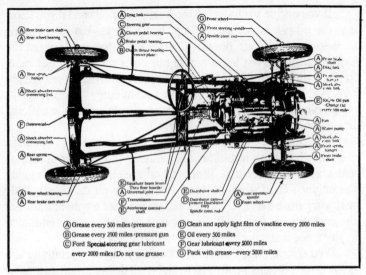

Fig. 16-1. Lubrication chart.

To service the chassis, raise the car on stands so that you can examine for wear, etc. Use a good quality grease or heavy oil as the lubrication chart indicates. Do not lubricate any rubber parts with grease. Use brake fluid for squeaks. Wipe the cups or grease fittings. Do not force dirt into the parts. If the universal joint has a place for a grease gun, grease lightly or you might blow the seals out. Some joints will have to be disassembled for lubrication.

Check the transmission and rear axle. If you have leaks, repair them and then use the proper lubricant. If the transmission is automatic, make sure that you use the proper make of transmission fluid or you will ruin the seals.

Lubricate engine accessories as required with oil or grease, but do it sparingly. Do not over lubricate the generator or starter. Pay attention to what the manufacturer is saying.

Fuel System

Depending on the style, keep the fuel system clean. See that the filters and traps are serviced. If you have the throw away type, replace the necessary ones at the fuel pump, in-line or at the carburetor. If the car has a *positive crankcase ventilation* (PCV) system, the valve is probably located in the valve cover. Remove it and shake it. If it rattles then it's okay (Fig. 16-2).

The air cleaner is easy to find and easy to service. This is especially true if it has a paper throw-away element. Oil-bath types should have the same type of oil as that used in the crankcase. Mesh-type filters can be washed and very lightly oiled.

While you are under the hood, check the outside condition of the radiator. If it is dirty, buggy or full of debris, use a garden hose to wash it clean from the opposite side from where the air enters. Straighten the cooling fins very carefully. Check the hoses. Replace them if they are soft or cracked.

See that the clamps are tight. Check the fan belt for cracks or peeling. Replace it before you have a problem. Adjust the tension if necessary and determine if the belt is okay. Check the radiator cap to see if it seals properly; if not, replace it.

See that the coolant level is all right and if it needs topping add antifreeze both for the rust inhibitor and for protection against freezing. If you suspect thermostat problems, replace the thermostat.

Two common problems are that the car heater does not produce enough heat or the engine takes a long time to reach operating temperature. Do some looking and catch these problems before you get out on the road. If you find that the coolant level is continually low, check for bubbles in the radiator. This could mean a cylinder head gasket leak. The engine must be running when you make this check.

To keep your car running at peak performance, the ignition system should be checked at least yearly. The points, condenser and spark plugs do the big job so see that they are in good condition. The rotor, cap and wiring must be corrosion free so that they can deliver the spark to the spark plugs.

See that the timing is all right. It must be checked every time the points are changed or adjusted. Use a timing light to check or a continuity to see when the points open in relation to the timing marks. When you are using the timing light, keep your hands clear of the fan blades. It just *looks* like the fan is turning slowly. Remember, the cost of cleaning spark plugs is hardly worth the effort.

Battery

To keep the starting and charging systems operating at peak efficiency, the battery must be kept in good shape. When the engine will not start, do not automatically blame the battery. It might be that the battery has been run down because the problem is in another system. I hope by now that you have purchased a battery hydrometer. One that has a thermometer on it would be the best.

Batteries that are sealed cannot be checked in any way. I'm assuming that most of you are still using the regular batteries instead of the maintenance-free ones. If you have one of the 'ball' type hydrometers, it is not as accurate as a "float" type, but it is easy to read. Do not add water to the battery before taking a reading. A reading of 1.260 indicates a fully charged battery, corrected for temperature. Readings of 1.150 or below indicate a dead cell.

If you are going to keep the battery terminals in good shape, it might be wise to purchase some battery cleaning tools. A pair of battery pliers or a short box-end wrench of the proper size is better than using your regular wrenches. Corrosion is a problem. A battery terminal puller and cleaning tool that will clean both cables and posts is about all you need.

Use a solution of baking soda and water to wash the battery case clean. If the cables are heavy with corrosion, sprinkle some baking soda on them. Let it work and then wash it off with water. Do the same for the hold-down bracket. Now loosen the battery bolts and pull the cable off. Clean the post and cable shiny clean. Use grease or petroleum jelly over the cable and post after you have put it back on. Check the cables. If they are in need of replacing, do so with ones of similar length and size. When you are replacing or cleaning, unhook the ground cable first. It is possible to get new ends for old cables, but unless the cable is in top shape it is wiser to replace the entire cable.

If you find that the battery is always thirsty and there are no visible leaks, this condition indicates that the battery is being overcharged. Low hydrometer readings can indicate that the battery is undercharged. The charging circuit will need attention. Use distilled water to bring the liquid level up to the desired mark. Batteries that are under charge produce explosive gasses, do not smoke while servicing them.

When using another battery to help the one you have in the car, if the one in the car has gone dead, use care that you don't blow them up. Do not connect the ground cable jumper to the battery. Connect it to a ground on the engine to prevent sparks. In case of acid contact, neutralize the area with water and seek medical help.

If the battery is in good condition, but the starter will not crank the engine, the starter will have to repaired or replaced. If the starter spins, but will not crank the engine, either the starter drive gear is damaged or the flywheel. Again the starter will have to be removed and the problem area inspected. If the starter is noisy, the

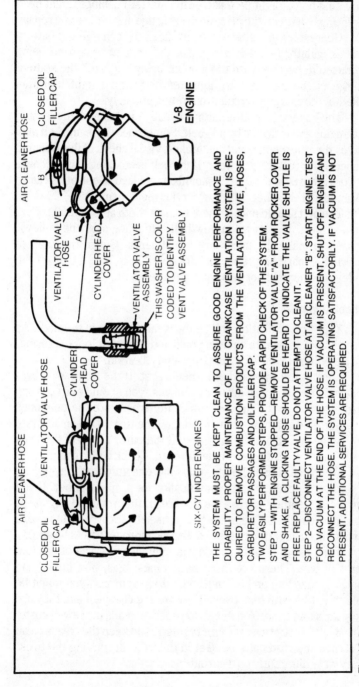

CLOSED OIL FILLER CAP

AIR CLEANER HOSE

B

VENTILATOR VALVE HOSE

A

CYLINDER HEAD COVER

VENTILATOR VALVE ASSEMBLY

THIS WASHER IS COLOR CODED TO IDENTIFY VENT VALVE ASSEMBLY

V-8 ENGINE

AIR CLEANER HOSE

VENTILATOR VALVE HOSE

CLOSED OIL FILLER CAP

CYLINDER HEAD COVER

SIX-CYLINDER ENGINES

THE SYSTEM MUST BE KEPT CLEAN TO ASSURE GOOD ENGINE PERFORMANCE AND DURABILITY. PROPER MAINTENANCE OF THE CRANKCASE VENTILATION SYSTEM IS REQUIRED TO REMOVE COMBUSTION PRODUCTS FROM THE VENTILATOR VALVE, HOSES, CARBURETOR PASSAGES AND OIL FILLER CAP.

TWO EASILY PERFORMED STEPS, PROVIDE A RAPID CHECK OF THE SYSTEM.

STEP 1—WITH ENGINE STOPPED—REMOVE VENTILATOR VALVE "A" FROM ROCKER COVER AND SHAKE. A CLICKING NOISE SHOULD BE HEARD TO INDICATE THE VALVE SHUTTLE IS FREE. REPLACE FAULTY VALVE, DO NOT ATTEMPT TO CLEAN IT.

STEP 2—DISCONNECT VENTILATOR VALVE HOSE AT AIR CLEANER "B". START ENGINE. TEST FOR VACUUM AT THE END OF THE HOSE. IF VACUUM IS PRESENT, SHUT OFF ENGINE AND RECONNECT THE HOSE. THE SYSTEM IS OPERATING SATISFACTORILY. IF VACUUM IS NOT PRESENT, ADDITIONAL SERVICES ARE REQUIRED.

Fig. 16-2. Location and service of PCV valve.

mounting bolts might be loose or the starter bushings might need replacing. Check on the price of an exchange unit before you repair.

Generators and alternators are used to recharge the battery and a regulator is used to regulate the amount of current being produced in balance with the amount being used and the state of charge of the battery. An ammeter or warning light indicates whether the charging circuit is operating properly.

The generator or alternator is usually located near the front of the engine and is driven by a V-belt. Sometimes this same belt also drives the water pump and fan. Make a visual check of this belt and inspect it for tension and wear. If the belt is cracking and the cover is worn away or separated, it should be replaced. Good belts can be adjusted if the bracket will allow for this movement.

The belt should not sag more than its width at the middle of the longest span. Do not pry a new belt into place over the pulleys. Loosen to make the necessary adjustments. Get in the habit of carrying a spare belt with you. Its possible to lose a belt off the pulleys and it might not be easy to get a new belt.

Wheel Alignment

Your first indication will be the wear patterns of the tires. As the problem gets more severe, you'll notice hard or loose steering, the car pulling to one side, and front-end vibration.

Look at the tires and the wheels first. If the tread wear bars appear in two or more adjacent grooves, you should start getting ready to replace the tires. If the center treads are the only ones wearing, this is a case of over inflating the tires. Use an accurate tire gauge and adjust the pressure. If the outer edges of the tires are wearing, then they are under inflated. Check with a gauge.

When one side of the tire wears more rapidly than the other, it should be checked at an alignment shop for proper camber. If you can feel a "feather" across the tire tread, the front end alignment should be checked. The problem is caused by incorrect alignment. A cupping wear pattern can be caused by improper wheel balance.

The type of driving you do will influence the type of tire that you will buy. There are three basic types: bias, bias belted and radial. Depending on how much you drive your car, you might be able to get by with bias tires. They are the cheapest and they are okay for short trips. You might consider retreads in view of costs. You should check tire pressure regularly and keep the treads clean of stones and road garbage. Get in the habit of rotating the tires. They wear differently on the front and the rear.

When you are servicing the front end, check for wear at the ball joints, control arm pivot points, steering linkage and tie-rod ends. You can check for worn shocks by bouncing each corner of the car up and down a few times. Let go and see how long it takes for the car to stop moving. If the shocks are good, the car shouldn't bounce more than once after you have let go. Repeat at each corner. Replace the shocks in pairs—front or rear. Do not get under the car to replace shocks unless the car is supported on stands. See that you get the proper replacement shocks.

Brakes, either mechanical or hydraulic, will need attention. Get in the habit of trying the brake pedal before you start the car. Afterward it might be too late. It's a sickening feeling when your foot is on the brake pedal all the way to the floorboards and the car merrily rolls along.

Mechanical brakes depend on mechanical advantage to assure maximum braking power. A twisted, bent or weak cross shaft will not deliver full pedal power to the brake. This result in hard pedal and uneven brakes. Lubricate all connections. Replace any parts that will cause lost motion and see that all the cotter pins are in place.

With hydraulic brakes, you must have fluid in the master cylinder. If you have to add fluid regularly, something is wrong with the system and it should be checked. On unmarked cylinders, keep the brake fluid level about one-fourth inch from the top. Fix any leaks at the wheel cylinders, flexible lines or solid, or at the master cylinder. Remove the drums to inspect linings. See that the adjuster mechanism moves freely and the springs are not distorted. Adjust the parking brake if necessary.

Check the front wheel bearings while you have the front drums off and service as required. Adjust bearing endplay and check wheel rotation.

Service to the drive line consists of proper lubrication to the various components as recommended by the manufacturers. The clutch pedal has the only adjustment that can be made without taking anything apart. This is the freeplay in the clutch pedal and it is easily adjusted by a threaded linkage. Allow about 1 inch on the pedal. Some throwout bearings have a lubrication line, but do not let any oil or grease get on the clutch linings.

Happy motoring.

Index